agenziax

2024, Agenzia X

Graphic Project
Antonio Boni

Cover Image
Paper Resistance • www.paper-resistance.org

Translation
Carmen Sorbara

Contacts
Agenzia X • via Giuseppe Ripamonti 13 • 20136 Milan
tel. 02/89401966
www.agenziax.it – info@agenziax.it
facebook.com/agenziax – instagram.com/agenziax

ISBN 978-88-95029-33-7

People who worked on this book...
Marco Philopat – editorial direction
Paoletta "Nevrosi" Mezza – editorial coordination

u.net

original
london style

hip hop, sound systems & black british culture

original
london style

Group photo during the screening of the documentary *Unstoppable* at the House of Vans, London, May 2016

Intro

London, 1988

It's the summer of 1988 and like many young Italians I'm in London for a summer language course. London so to speak, as school and home are in fact in Woodford and Loughton in a very suburban area, almost on the Essex border. I practically live in the countryside, but from the moment I landed my mind belongs to the centre of the city, precisely the West End. There is Groove Records there, the object or, better, the place of my desires: a Rap record shop located in Greek Street, Soho. It was recommended to me by a mate of the Einstein School who had happened there by chance the previous summer. At that time it was considered the record shop par excellence, it had all the latest Rap records imported from the United States. As far as I knew, it was a very small shop where, once its threshold was crossed, I would have found a middle-aged lady able to give me all the necessary tips I needed.

Only by going there I would find out that the small size of the shop meant waiting in endless queues, especially on Saturday afternoons. Right at the entrance, hanging from the wall, there was the Future Rap Chart drawn up by Tim Westwood. At the time, I had no idea of who he was but his chart hanging there gave me the impression of being something important. However, for a sixteen year-old boy like me who was born and raised in the southern suburbs of Milan, even just the subway journey to Soho admiring that human sample which was so different from the one I was used to, it was as good as the destination.

And the Soho of the 1980s was not certainly the same of 2022: sex shops, strip clubs, pubs, romantics and dreamers, drunks, prostitutes and fools of all sorts. The streets were different every day, empty lots, buildings in ruins, punks, skins and all the different urban tribes, each one with its own distinctive signs. The opportunity for the first "escape" had arisen thanks to another friend and high schoolmate, Fritz, who was also in London for a language course, but with his parents in tow. We had arranged to meet in Covent Garden, in the heart of the West End, in front of the Opera House.

The following Friday, after class, I rode the usual train and instead of getting off at Woodford, I continued on the red line transferring at Holborn, arriving at my destination just after one stop on the blue line.

I am early and so I sit and wait on the steps of the theatre. In front of me I see Black kids dancing on a piece of linoleum, performing for the tourists who gather around them one after another, drawn in by the music coming out from their dual cassette boombox. I am fascinated; I have never seen anything like that before. Before I even have the time to recover, another performance begins. A duo is performing: they dance strangely and jerky, with rapid muscle contraction, moving in perfect harmony with the music. They look like robots experiencing the consequences of a short circuit.

Fritz, who had meanwhile sat down beside me to watch, tells me he has seen similar things in Milan, at Il Muretto, in Galleria Vittorio Emanuele. For me, however, it's something completely new. A couple of years earlier I had watched some of the first Rap music videos, Walk This Way by RUN DMC and Fight For Your Right by the Beastie Boys. Then, a friend had recorded a series of ninety-minute cassette tapes with the hits of the main Rap groups of that time.

I was learning how to recognize that rough sound. I loved Rap music and could spend days and days looking at album covers, trying to grasp the smallest details in order to understand the aesthetics. However, at the time, I knew almost nothing about Breaking and Writing.

We are about to leave, heading towards Groove Records, when the two girls sitting next to us start a conversation, inviting us to stay seated as the dancer who is about to perform is Danny Francis, apparently one of the best Poppers in all of London.

I start to doubt whether it's just an excuse to strike up a conversation. They begin talking non-stop, and within a few minutes they explain the dynamics of that location, which, according to what they say, is the meeting point of the best MCs, DJs, B-Boys and Writers of the city and beyond! In essence, it's like the Mecca of the London Hip Hop scene. It feels surreal to me: on my first day of complete autonomy I just discovered the nerve centre of London's Hip Hop and I also found a guide in the guise of a b-girl. I also learned that Covent Garden is the only place in the entire city where busking, or performing for money, is allowed and this is why several dancers and crews moved to the West End, the same area where the police do not take kindly to the presence of young Black people. I also discovered that most of the graffiti on the billboards around the Opera House are by the Chrome Angelz, the crew of the legendary Mode2..

The two girls, so ready to share those stories with us, are dressed alike: same tracksuit jackets, t-shirts, denims and Adidas Superstar. The only difference is the name on their belt buckle, the so-called name belt. The one I like is named Karen. We spend the rest of the afternoon and part of the evening with them, all four of us sitting on those same steps, chatting away. At the time to say goodbye Karen gave me her phone number, telling me to call her as she wants to show me the way to Groove Records. She didn't need to tell me twice. The next morning I called her and in the early afternoon we met at Tottenham Court Road and made our way to Greek Street. I spent a long time with her over the next two weeks and almost every day I found an excuse to break away from the group of the Italian students and join her. Next stop: West End. Destination: adventure. Thanks to Karen, I discovered a lot about London, its locations and the main characters of its urban Hip Hop scene.

London, 2009

I walk along Brick Lane, one of the most famous streets in East London that connects Whitechapel High Road to Bethnal Green Road, passing through Spitalfields. The area is also known as BanglaTown due to its many Asian restaurants located there. Brick Lane is a very popular street for tourists and Londoners, but it hasn't always been that way. A popular saying, in fact, claims that every stolen bicycle in the city can be found for sale at the Brick Lane market. Nowadays, the area is known both for graffiti and street art, as well as for its flea markets and vintage shops selling records, books and clothing. I'm looking for the Vibe Bar, where this afternoon the King of the Beats event will take place: it's a competition between Hip Hop beatmakers, organised by Pritt Kalsi, filmmaker and music producer. The evening's program includes the appearance of a guest from the United States, Mikey D (Mikey D and the LA Posse and Main Source), along with many protagonists of the Hip Hop scene: starting with the event's host, Sparkii Ski, old school beatmaker and member of the Jus Bad Crew. With him, on the ones and twos, there will be DJ Pogo and DJ Devastate (of Demon Boyz), both DJs and beatmakers with several records to their credit that have become classics in the British Hip Hop scene. The beatmakers competition has pretty simple rules: they offered a budget of £15 to every participant in order to buy some vinyl records they will use for sampling and building a beat. Everything must be done within a maximum of twenty-four hours.

Mikey D is a MC who grew artistically in the streets and jams of Queens, becoming popular battle after battle. In 1988, he won the MC competition at the New Music Seminar. In an era where eclecticism and originality were considered as the sacraments, the competition as the holy spirit of that religion, and the battles represented the altar where to celebrate that ritual. The New Music Seminar was one of the biggest events at the time and right now I'm here to interview Mikey D for the chapter of my book Louder than a Bomb, dedicated to international battles.

The previous evening, we had dinner together and came to an agreement for an interview before the beginning of the event, which is why I arrived at the location while everything was still being set up. We sat in a room behind the stage, engaged in a passionate conversation. He tells me about his win and the following and unexpected battle against Grandmaster Melle Mel, one of his idols. At that moment, another voice interrupts the story: "I was there too, along with the Covent Garden crew. I remember it all as if it were yesterday". I turn around and, surprisingly, there are at least five other people sitting around us. His story was so intense, full of details and anecdotes that I didn't notice anything else. For their part, those present had all been in religious silence until that moment, but within a few seconds, however, the interview took a different turn, becoming a collective conversation. Intrigued by the situation, I decided to place the tape recorder on the table in the middle of the room so as not to miss a single word of that dialogue.

Throughout the afternoon, I would discover that those individuals were some of the most prominent names of the Old school British Hip Hop scene: MC Mello, DJ Pogo, DJ Devastate and Cutmaster Swift, who himself won the New Music Seminar in 1989 in the DJ category.

The words of MC Mello, his memories about that historic battle in 1988, his reflections from the perspective of the audience, from beneath the stage, were complementary to those told by Mikey D, from above the stage. The contrast of different memories and points of view would lead me to shift my attention towards topics that I hadn't paid much attention to. I had studied about artists, Rap records and their social and cultural impact in the United States for years but I had never asked myself that same question about Europe. What

DJ Devastate and DJ Pogo on the turntables during the King of the Beats event

had been the impact of the first Rap records or the first books and films that talked about all of it on young people? In my mind, Mikey D represented the US Rap production while Mello, from below the stage and his position of subordination, represented Europe. USA vs EU. That afternoon the Flip the Script project was born, a focus on the Hip Hop scenes of five European capital cities. Later it became *Unstoppable*, a documentary about the roots of the Hip Hop scene in London, and eventually transformed into the book you hold now in your hands: Original London Style, an oral history about Hip Hop, sound systems and Black British culture.

In 1986 I could never have imagined that thirty years later I would return to Covent Garden looking for those same – back then – young people.

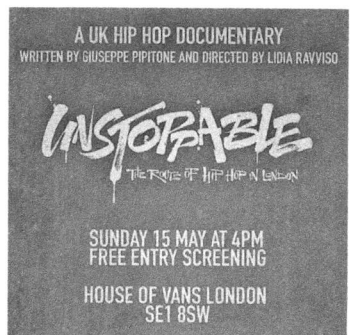

A UK HIP HOP DOCUMENTARY
WRITTEN BY GIUSEPPE PIPITONE AND DIRECTED BY LIDIA RAVVISO

INSTOPPABLE
THE ROUTE OF HIP HOP IN LONDON

SUNDAY 15 MAY AT 4PM
FREE ENTRY SCREENING

HOUSE OF VANS LONDON
SE1 8SW

Poster for the screening of
Unstoppable in London, May 2016

London 2013

The online crowdfunding and the DJ sets organised at Cox18 in Milan and at Forte Prenestino in Rome allowed us to raise the necessary funds for a month of filming in London. Yesterday, we spent the entire day in Ladbroke Grove, in the west area of the city: one of the most fascinating spots of the English capital, a true cultural hotspot and a meeting point for different ethnicities, with a strong Caribbean community. Over the years, the neighbourhood had witnessed protests and riots, but also for relevant artistic and literary experiences. Some of the most interesting bands were born right here and made reference to this area in their imagery, and I am talking about iconic groups like Aswad and The Clash. It is the area where Duke Vin turned on the first sound system in 1955. It is also the location of the annual Notting Hill Carnival, which takes place on the third weekend of August during the Bank holiday: a two-day street party filled with music, food and the celebration of Caribbean culture.

The location of the interview is a park at the foot of a grey tower, so hideous that it reminds me of a warehouse for human bodies. Here, one can find one of the city's first and most renowned Hall of Fames. Ladbroke Grove is known in

Hip Hop historiography as the birthplace of one of the early London crews: the Krew, spelled with a K to differentiate it from the American word. In that park, I met two of its most renowned members: Skam One, a legendary b-boy and writer, and Sir Drew, a MC who along with DJ Newtrament and Monoman, was famous for releasing the first UK Rap record, London Bridge is Falling Down in 1982. I also met Dizzi Heights, the MC who published *Christmas Rapping*, a record that, according to some, contends for primacy with DJ Newtrament.

Dizzi actually lived in that dreadful building. Their stories about the roots of Hip Hop in London take me back in time during the late '70s and early '80s, a turbulent era characterised by frequent protests, strikes and a strong racist element.

In such an uncertain social framework, London also becomes the birthplace of numerous subcultures that flourish in the most disparate ways and places.

From the Rastafarian community in Notting Hill to the Punks in King's Road, the Rockabilly Culture in Elephant & Castle and the New Wave movement at the Blitz Club in Covent Garden: the streets of London were filled with a wave of creative energy. Moreover, the first half of the '80s represented a crucial turning point for all the music production technologies: synthesisers, samplers, sequencers and drum machines became more affordable and accessible, allowing for experimentation and the pursuit of a different sound.

To interview Jonzi D, b-boy, choreographer and founder of Breaking Convention, I make my way to Bow, in the East End of the city. As the son of immigrants from the Barbados islands, Jonzi enjoys joking about his British, or rather Cockney origins, as he was born and raised in that very neighbourhood.

The typical London expression *Born within the sound of the Bow Bells*, referring to the sound of the bells of St. Mary-le-Bow church, identifies both the working-class layers of the eastern area of the city (Cockney) and the local city slang (also Cockney). With Jonzi D, I discuss how Sound System culture, inherited from the vibrant community of Caribbean immigrants, has shaped the evolution of British Hip Hop from its inception. Sound systems are a kind of mobile disco imported from the ghettos of Kingston in the 1950s, thanks to the pioneering soundmen like Duke Vin and Count Suckle.

They have always represented both a source of celebration and a catalyst for change. Actually, their proliferation has provided entertainment and aggregation for the Black community, and their popularity in the poorer areas has laid the groundwork for linking music and social reality. Starting from the 1960s, they were present in all English cities, modelled after the Jamaican style, and they spread by imitating the basic elements that were essentially the same. However, in the British context, those itinerant discos would venture into new sound territories, conquering top positions in the national charts.

UK Rap, Jungle, Drum'n'Bass and Dubstep, up to Grime music and beyond, have all their roots traced back to sound system culture. The children and grandchildren of the Windrush generation, artists like Rodney P, Jazzie B, Daddy G, Congo Natty, Hollie Cook and Wiley were once young disciples of this youth culture. And if their love for the powerful bass originated with sound systems, surely that passion led them to transcend its boundaries, creating new genres. These artists represent a direct testament to the legacy that Jamaica has passed on to the world: walls of loudspeakers, powerful

Dolby D and U.net in the West End, London 2013

bass and lyrics with strong social content. Although sound systems originated in Jamaica, it is in the UK that they have become part of the global musical culture.

I met the legendary Dolby D, b-boy of the London All Star crew, and MC Mello in the West End as they will be my special guides in a kind of a walking tour. We spend four hours together exploring the most significant places of the first Hip Hop scene, retracing the typical day of an '80s b-boy. We started from Spats in Oxford Street, the first London Hip Hop club, and we passed by Greek Street, where Groove Records once was, which is now turned into a vintage clothing shop. We arrived at the Africa Centre where in the second half of the 1980s every saturday night you could find Jazzie B on the ones and twos along with his crew named Soul II

Soul. We pass Covent Garden where Dolby challenged the whole Rock Steady Crew on his own, and by The Centre, the youth centre in Saint Martin-in-the-Fields, a refuge for those young people during the cold winter days, and finally we reach the subway underpass in Charing Cross, where there is a corridor covered with mirrors along its length, used by b-boys to be able to watch themselves in action, just like in a dance school.

Thirty years later, MC Mello, who at the time was a popper and known as Moomin, tries out a few moves in front of those mirrors. His words have a nostalgic flavour, as if he is talking about the best years of his life. He also remembers that it was right there where he would fix his jheri curl – his curly hair – so fashionable at the time, to always look sharp or, as they would say in America, fresh. In that scenario, both of them emphasise how Hip Hop began to make its way with its disciplines but dancing and writing were trailblazers, claiming urban spaces and redefining the social geography of the city. The conquest of a public place in the city centre, like Covent Garden, was perhaps the most striking example of the ongoing transformation. To better understand the stories of the pioneers it was crucial to grasp what was happening around them as Black youth cultures, precisely because they are black and have always been subjected to ghettoization. Those young people had responded to marginalisation by envisioning new creative strategies, and music had played a central role because it has always had the power to transport us to another dimension without regard to gender, class or race. From early neighbourhood parties in community centres, the scene had started to spread throughout the city, eventually reaching the centre, effectively transforming it into the main gathering place for all Hip Hop enthusiasts.

And as MC Mello talks about it, his words become poetry: "Covent Garden represented the heart, the fulcrum of the situation. The place to be for those who loved breaking, graffiti and Rap...".

I met Rodney P, who is considered the godfather of UK Hip Hop, at the entrance of Battersea Park, on the southern side of the river Thames, not far from the city centre. Arriving by bus, it is impossible not to notice the silhouette of the now famous power plant portrayed on the cover of Pink Floyd's album Animals, as well as on the cover of the Beatles and The Who, and seen in many videos and TV series.

Battersea Park was a meeting point for many young people from South London. It was in this park that MCs and DJs like Mello, Kamanchi Sly (Hijack) and the same Rodney P took their first steps. Initially, they went to the park as box boys – the way they called the workers responsible for carrying the equipment of local sound systems – but over time they had also tried to take the microphone. It was there that they learned the fundamentals of Reggae-style Toasting, elements that would later be very useful also for Rap music.

Rodney P, together with Bionic, were the two MCs of the London Posse and changed the face and history of British Hip Hop, introducing a distinctly London slang and sound. Just by putting one of their records on the turntable you can grasp the entire legacy of the Reggae sound system scene. For example Money Mad, the first attempt at a raw fusion between Rap and Reggae, is the song that inaugurates the UK Rap scene. When talking about his early sources of inspiration, Rodney P mentions some American MCs but, above all, English toasters; he also talks about the Saxon Sound parties in Lewisham. He goes on mentioning Peter King with his Fast Chat style and Smiley Culture's Cockney

Translation, one of the first examples where black and white slang appear side by side in a song – although still distinct from each other. Rodney also tells me that Money Mad was the Hip Hop version of a track called Inner Cities by another UK toaster, Tenor Fly.

Rodney P talks about his decision to rap with the same language he used every day, blending Jamaican street slang and London slang. It is hard to explain how significant this transition was, especially now that all the British MCs rap with their own accent, but it further highlights the legacy left by the London Posse. Spending several hours together, I realise that his attitude, always kind and friendly, conveys a sense of respect and, if I had known many stories that I would discover later, I would have also added a certain awe.

That calmness that shines through his slow stride hides years of street life filled with performances and illicit activities. I remember smiling while reading a post with a fan's testimony, who was under the stage and went from singing every line of his favourite group's song while showing off a gold chain, one of those massive chains so fashionable in those days, to running away chased by his own idols who wanted to steal it. There is no wonder if you think that Bionic in Money Mad raps: "I make it easy, or you can get it hard / gimme your money, your jewellery and your credit card".

Somehow, I'm glad I met him in Battersea in 2013 rather than Covent Garden in 1986!

In the following days I met Susie Q and MC Remedee also known as the Cookie Crew, in a park in Clapham Junction, South London; then DJ Devastate of the Demon Boys in Tottenham and, in the same North London area, DJ Fingers, in Seven Sisters. The interviews followed one after the other and they all enthusiastically responded to our invitation. We try to meet them in their neighbourhoods, in their stomping ground, those places where they took their first steps, thus also creating a sort of social map linked to the origins of Hip Hop in London.

From parks to community centres, pirate radios to record stores, clothing shops to clubs. The London that I face has distinct characteristics and references, very different from any other depiction of the city. From the suburbs to the centre, I'm riding the wave of a creative surge that laid the foundations of a multicultural movement capable of redesigning popular English culture.

Harvard 2019

The day of my colloquium speech at Harvard has arrived. I have prepared by studying for ten hours a day over the past two months. The audience that I will face represents a real challenge, as there are some of the most influential names of the American academic scene, starting with Henry Louis Gates Jr., director of the Department of African and African-American Studies, and Marcyliena Morgan, Director of the Hip Hop Archive. There will also be Cornel West, Murray Forman and Bakari Kitwana. I have been awarded the NAS Fellowship, a scholarship established in 2013 and sponsored by the rapper NAS, thanks to the editorial project of Original London Style. And now I'm here in Cambridge, across the Charles River compared to Boston, with the opportunity to study for a year at the Hip Hop Archive & Research Institute, located within the Hutchins Center at Harvard.

In a reality like this, light years away from my daily life, the first thing that comes to my mind every morning when entering the historic university campus is that bar where Notorious BIG raps: "You never thought that Hip Hop would take it this far".

In Juicy, Notorious BIG talks about how his life changed thanks to Rap music, and I can fully relate to it in my own way. I could have never imagined studying at Harvard, thanks to a fellowship paid by a rapper. After years of field research, I had to take a break to delve deeper into the historical trajectory of Black British culture, in order to integrate it with the interviews and the documentation that I had already collected. The idea was also to understand how Black music in England transitioned from being perceived as a mere import from abroad to becoming such a significant presence that even a conservative media such as the BBC has dedicated an ad hoc digital channel to it. As Black music evolved, encompassing Calypso and Jazz, Reggae and Hip Hop, Grime and Afrobeat, even the artists themselves transitioned from being disparaged as immigrants, to being proudly recognized as British, even by the mainstream. We talk about a time span of almost seventy years, from Lord Kitchener stepping off the Windrush ship in 1948 and singing "London is the place for me...", to the rapper Tinie Tempah in 2011 comfortably sitting on Breakfast TV couch and giving advice on which tea is best to use with London water (Yorkshire Gold, according to the artist).

Although there were already small communities and black professionals since the early 20th century, this story officially begins after World War II, with the arrival of the Empire Windrush ship in the Tilbury Docks. For the reconstruction of the country, which was desired and supported by the government, the workforce was recruited from the former colonies. The men and women who set sail from the Caribbean Islands hoped to find what they had been taught to consider as their motherland. They departed as Commonwealth citizens, but landed as immigrants placed at the bottom ring of the social ladder. At that time, no one could have imagined the deep impact that moment would have on reshaping British culture in the following decades. The music associated with that initial phase was Calypso, a genre coming from Trinidad, which was most fitting to depict the mix of hope and disillusionment that characterised the experiences of the early migrants.

In the 1960s, the British government put a halt to immigration, considering it as a threat to the English Way of Life, as evoked by Enoch Powell in 1968 in his Rivers of Blood speech, in which the Conservative parliamentarian argued that the country could no longer afford such a flow of migration and proposed repatriation as a solution. The response of the Black community did not wait long. The impetus for politicisation came from the African American liberation movement, particularly from the H.P. Newton's Black Panthers. The soundtrack of that decade came from Jamaica, with the rhythms of Ska, Rocksteady and later Reggae music.

The 1970s began with a devastating economic crisis, while the government and the press contributed to exacerbating the dichotomy between foreigners and citizens, supporting what became known as common sense racism.

Precisely in this period, new youth cultures emerged, attempting to mend the social fracture that had been created, and once again, music would be the chosen weapon to resist the status quo and articulate an alternative model of coexistence.

In 1979, under the Conservative government of Margaret Thatcher, a period of intense conflict began, marked by numerous racist attacks and episodes of police brutality, which culminated in the urban riots in 1981. Between the mid-1970s and the 1980s, a Black British counterculture emerged, attempting to redefine forms of resistance and negotiate a new collective identity within a complex system of relationships between family culture, national identity, local dimension, and global influences from the United States, Jamaica and the African continent. The popularity of Rastafarian ideas, the influence of black power movements, and the rediscovery of African roots are the essential steps in a process that leads to an artistic synthesis, especially in the music fields, which will dominate the imagination throughout the 1980s and beyond.

Some texts by historians and scholars have provided me with the necessary tools for my research: Black British Culture and Society: A Text Reader by Kwesi Owusu, Resistance Through Rituals: Youth Subcultures in Post-War Britain by Stuart Hall and Tony Jefferson, There Ain't No Blacks in the Union Jack and The Black Atlantic by Paul Gilroy, Cut 'n' Mix by Dick Hebdige, New Ethnicities and Urban Culture by Les Back, Black Culture, White Youth by Simon Jones, It's a London Thing, by Caspar Melville, Sounds Like London and Bass Culture by Lloyd Bradley, just to name a few ones of the key works.

October 2021

I'm back in Blighty. Back to London. Still in the south of the city, in Lewisham. I walk through the streets of the neighbourhood with Tippa Irie, a legendary DJ (an MC in Hip Hop) from Saxon Sound, a sound system that originated in that area in 1976 thanks to Lloyd "Musclehead" Francis and Denis Rowe.

Lewisham is also the neighbourhood where Jah Shaka, operator of the homonymous sound system, opened his record shop and label, Fay Music. It is also where the Moonshot Youth Club was located, then raided and vandalised by the police in 1975, in one of the many episodes of brutality that fueled the tensions leading up to the Lewisham Battle in 1977. On that occasion, the National Front's attempt to march from New Cross to Lewisham was disrupted by black organisations and anti-fascist groups.

It was in that neighbourhood that the tragic incident known as the New Cross Massacre occurred, where a fire during a house party resulted in the deaths of thirteen young people. It was also the target of racist attacks by the National Front and other fascist groups. Lewisham is also the place where Peter King, DJ of the Saxon Crew, creates the Toasting style known as Fast Chat in 1982, during the party called DJ Jamboree Dance. This style had illustrious antecedents in Jamaican artists such as U-Roy, Brigadier Jerry and Nicodemus, but in London it was reworked from a strictly Black British perspective. The history of the birth of this stylistic innovation was immortalised in the track Fast Style Origination by Asher Senator, another DJ by Saxon Sound. Tippa Irie tells me about the tensions of those days, and his memories are still very vivid. He also talks about the stylistic innovations of the Saxon Sound DJs and emphasises that their parties were a celebration of joy, but they were also spaces where people could reaffirm unity and Black autonomy. Babylon, the film by director Franco Rosso released in 1980, is perhaps the most fitting example to understand what has just been written. It is no coincidence that it was filmed in Deptford, a district in Lewisham. Tippa strives to make me understand how those parties were spaces where pleasure and politics

Tippa Irie and U.net in Lewisham, London 2021

coexisted. And here there is the real innovation introduced by Saxon: their lyrics represented the voice of the street, of the common people, just like Daddy Colonel, another DJ of the crew, sang "with the Saxon Posse now, we chat what's happening here, not Jamaica, America or Timbuktu". Living in a reality that pushed towards marginalisation every day, where the fear of racist violence was a persistent threat, has undoubtedly led those MCs to express their anxieties and frustrations on the microphone, but also hope and joy for a different future.

Singing about issues related to the English reality it became almost natural to express themselves using a combination of cockney and patois, just as they did every day. That choice highlighted the dual role they were forced to play, dealing with institutions, their own family and community, with teachers and police on one side, and friends and relatives on the other.

Fast Chat not only represented a stylistic but also a content innovation, as it allowed those DJs to express themselves in a unique way, mixing local and global influences with technological advancements, transforming themselves and their stories into an irresistible art form.

Tippa Irie is an incredible character and I should have filmed that interview. To make me understand what he was saying about the evolution of Toasting he started singing some songs, highlighting the different styles and key elements. It was a real lesson about the art of Toasting.

I'm heading to Brixton to meet another iconic character of the Reggae scene, Festus, the selector of Sir Coxsone Sound System since 1965. I can't wait to go over the genres and records he played in the course of over fifty years of career. Most of the questions I will ask him are related to Lovers Rock, one of the earliest versions of indigenous Reggae that his sound system popularised starting from the late '70s.

We agreed that I would call him once I arrived at the subway station but when I did it, I unfortunately discovered that the interview was cancelled due to Covid: his daughter has tested positive and he is in quarantine.

I'm sure I will have the opportunity to meet him on another occasion but I'm really sorry I was not able to enter his memories and reflections in Original London Style.

Milan, 2022

I'm writing the introduction to this book, and to find the right inspiration, I'm watching some Uk Rap videos of the artists I've been enjoying lately: Stormzy, Dave, Skepta, Giggs, and my absolute favourite, Little Simz. The British music scene continues to evolve, taking on mixed identities and hybrid sounds that are the result from a constant negotiation between external influences, internal needs and technological innovations. Music remains today one of the favourite tools for young people to articulate social criticisms and grievances, but also to party and dance until dawn. With influences from the entire diaspora, this music captures the hybrid essence of the Black British culture.

A hybrid and ever-evolving essence, that's where much of the charm of this city comes from. I remember well how, while walking through the different neighbourhoods over the past ten years, I have witnessed the consolidation of other slangs. Not only slang, but also colours, scents and flavours that alternated, followed one another, and merged together. Migration flows have produced such changes that the African component has become the preponderant one in the Black diaspora. Today, second or third generation migrants in big cities like London and Manchester have started celebrating their roots gaining an increasingly larger audience.

For decades, British Black music has been dominated by the sound imported from the Caribbean and the United States, giving rise to different youth cultures such as Lovers Rock, Fast Chat, UK Rap and later Jungle, Garage and Grime. However, now the most popular music in the UK charts is Afrobashment, also known as Afro Trap, Afro Swing or Afro Hop. The characteristics of this new genre combine elements of Ghanaian and Nigerian Afrobeat, Jamaican Dancehall, Rap, as well as Atlanta Trap or the Chicago Drill, blending different slangs: Pidgin English with Patois, Creole with Lingala and Cockney. Since 2011, the release year of J Hus debut album, a new generation of Black artists has been rewriting the rules of music, once again highlighting both the uniqueness and the complexity of Black British culture.

Artists Featured in the Oral History

Alex Mac ▶ writer.

Basil ▶ b-boy, one of the first street dancers in Covent Garden.

Buddha Stephen Leafloor ▶ educator and member of the Canadian Floor Masters.

Bunny Bread ▶ DJ, writer and photographer.

Cookie Crew (MC Remedee & Susie Q) ▶ one of the first all-female Mc crews.

Cutmaster Swift ▶ DJ and member of the Imperial Mixers crew, winner of the DMC in 1989.

Dave Vj ▶ DJ and member of the Mastermind Roadshow crew.

Dizzi Heights ▶ London-based Mc and producer.

DJ Devastate ▶ DJ, producer, and member of the Demon Boyz and The Firm.

DJ Fingers ▶ London-based DJ, producer, and member of Sindecut.

DJ Newtrament ▶ DJ credited for releasing the first UK rap record, "London Bridge Is Falling Down," and forming the first London hip-hop sound system, Rock Box.

DJ Pogo ▶ DJ, London-based producer, and member of the Jus Badd Crew.

DJ Supreme ▶ DJ, producer, and member of the Hijack group.

Dolby D ▶ pioneer of b-boying in the London scene and member of the London All Star.

Family Quest MCs ▶ Cheeko, Dirty Harry, Mc E=mix, and Mystery Mc are the Mcs of one of the first London rap crews.

Greg Wilson ▶ DJ, music producer, and writer.

Linton Lee ▶ DJ, producer, and member of the Faze One group.

Fraggle ▶ one of the earliest b-boys in Covent Garden.

Fresh Ski ▶ MC.

Gordon Mac ▶ DJ and founder of the pirate radio station Kiss FM.

Greg Wilson ▶ DJ and electro producer.

Ishmahil Blagrove ▶ activist and documentary and author.

James McNally ▶ former journalist for the historic English magazine "Hip Hop Connection".

Jonzi D ▶ MC, b-boy, and founder of Breaking Convention.

Mekka DBC ▶ promoter and DJ of the pirate radio Dread Broadcasting Corporation.

Murray Forman ▶ author and professor at Northwestern University.

MC Duke ▶ b-boy and Mc.

MC Mello ▶ body popper and Mc.

Pride ▶ writer and member of the legendary Chrome Angelz crew.

Rodney P ▶ Mc of the London Posse.

Simon Jones ▶ academic professor and author of the books *Scientists of Sound* and *Black Culture, White Youth*.

Simon Harris ▶ DJ, producer, and founder of the Music of Life label.

Simon Reynolds ▶ music journalist and author of numerous books on countercultures.

Sir Drew ▶ Mc who rapped on the first UK rap record, *London Bridge Is Falling Down*.

Skam One ▶ writer and member of one of the first crews in London, Krew.

Sparkii Ski ▶ music producer and member of the Jus Badd Crew.

Tippa Irie ▶ MC of the legendary Saxon Sound crew.

Yankee ▶ beatboxer, part of the first Covent Garden scene.

Cited Interviews

Bionic ▶ MC of the London Posse.

Don Letts ▶ DJ and author.

Fab Five Freddy ▶ Host, writer, Mc, and director.

Futura ▶ legendary old-school American writer.

Malcolm McLaren ▶ manager, music producer, and more.

Morgan Khan ▶ founder of the Street Sounds label.

Norman Jay ▶ DJ, author, and radio speaker, awarded the title Member of the British Empire for contributions to culture in the UK.

Jay Strongman ▶ English DJ and writer.

Jazzie B ▶ DJ, music producer, and founder of the Soul II Soul collective.

Terry Farley ▶ English DJ and music producer.

GLC'S GIANT OPEN AIR
BREAK DANCE FESTIVA

FREE

JUBILEE GARDENS
SOUTH BANK

SUNDAY
9 SEPTEMBER
2-8 PM

DJ-TIM WESTWOOD
WITH THE
NATION'S TOP:
★ **DANCE CREWS**
★ **RAP CREWS**
★ **SCRATCH/MIX-DJ's**

STREET HOCKEY, FREESTYLE HULA-HOOPIN
EXHIBITION, JB ROADSHOW, PHASE 1
ROADSHOW, FUNFAIR, FOOD ON SALE
ALL DANCE CREWS WELCOME
COMPETITION PRIZES
FOR FURTHER INFORMATION
PHONE 633-5824

Early stages

Hip Hop Goes International

The story of the origins of Hip Hop is well known by now, there are several books and documentaries written by artists, scholars, academics and journalists who have told it from different perspectives. A story that has become almost an urban legend, turning the pioneers of the scene into true pop icons. The first signs of this cultural revolution were observed in the early 1970s, in that dangerous and inaccessible no-man's land, where crime and chaos were the norm, known as the *Boogie Down Bronx*.

During that time, while a deep recession was strangling the American economy and the city of New York itself was on the brink of bankruptcy, the streets of the most deteriorated neighbourhoods seemed to be simmering with a wave of creative energy. Not only that. Despite the social shock resulting directly from misguided municipal policies, such as *Urban Renewal* plans and the flight of the richest white components to the suburbs, a new social ferment was emerging, especially in the Bronx.

The distance between white neighbourhoods and the predominantly Black and Latino urban centres became progressively wider. What was happening in these urban spaces, on the street corners, in public parks and in basements, would provide marginalised youth with significant expressive opportunities and the birth of new art forms that would, within a few years, transform into a multi-million dollar industry.

In a short period of time, the Hip Hop scene had developed a complex communication network through tapes recorded by DJs, played on the streets by powerful boomboxes that circulated throughout New York. Thanks to those cassette tapes sent to relatives outside the City and carried overseas by the military, Rap music was crossing the borders. The Bronx taxis, reminiscent of the train drivers who had distributed blues records years earlier, helped to fuel its popularity. The circulation of the first cassette tapes allowed the music to travel, thus involving many followers and admirers. The enormous popularity of the artists made it almost inevitable that some independent entrepreneurs would try to exploit that new musical genre.

1979 was the year when Hip Hop culture, once invisible to most, emerged from the underground and began to conquer the whole world. In fact, it was in that year that the debut single of the newly formed Sugar Hill Records, *Rapper's Delight* by the Sugar Hill Gang, was released.

The song became a huge success, selling over two million copies and reaching number four on the R&B chart and thirty-six on the pop chart, making it the best-selling twelve-inch record in the world.

While there had been previous attempts to release rap records, there is no doubt that *Rapper's Delight* was the first song to achieve tremendous success. Sylvia Robinson, former singer and one of the first women to become a music producer and founder of a record label, produced and recorded the song, fulfilling a dream she had been pursuing for years. For a long time, she had been trying to release a Rap record, getting mostly sceptical responses by the insiders of the music industry, so she decided to do it herself. The Sugarhill Gang was a studio creation that had never performed live. *Rapper's Delight* was conceived with the explicit goal of creating a success that would be accessible to a wide audience who knew nothing about Hip Hop music or the Bronx.

The totally improvised song, which lasts sixteen minutes, has only one predefined bar in the intro in which Wonder Mike says "What you hear is not a test, I'm rapping to the beat", anticipating to the world the musical revolution that would hit it shortly. *Rapper's Delight* arrived in the UK to be played in clubs by only a handful of DJs, like most of the dance and R&B singles from the United States that became popular thanks to their success on the dancefloor. Usually, radio stations would only play those songs when they were already climbing the charts. The same happened with *Rapper's Delight*, which reached number three on the UK singles chart in December, 1979.

On the 6th of that month, the Sugarhill Gang reached the peak of their popularity when they were invited to perform on the most popular music program of the BBC, *Top of the Pops*. For most international artists, appearing on the BBC Television Centre was a must as the show, with its 19

The Sugar Hill Gang during their performance on the TV program *Top of the Pops*, London 1979

million viewers, provided extremely high visibility. The day the three MCs performed on the show marked the debut of Simon Bates, who was already known as film director and radio personality, as a television host. On that occasion, due to the excitement of his first appearance, Bates made a series of monstrous gaffes and could not get anything right. Not to mention the horrible sweater he was wearing. When introducing the song, he referred to it as *The Rapper*. The mistake was likely derived from an attempt to describe the role of the MC rather than the song itself, as if he considered them as aliens from another galaxy. Despite that glaring mistake, the group's performance struck like an explosion the imagination of thousands of boys and girls throughout England.

DJ Pogo ▶ It came out in the summer of '79. When my sisters and I heard *Rapper's Delight*, we thought it was *Good Time* by Chic, which was a big disco record at the time. But when I heard rappin' on it, I was like wow what is this?

Bunny Bread ▶ In 1979, *Rapper's Delight* came out, and we heard the lyrics "Hip Hop the hippie the hippie to the Hip Hip Hop and you don't stop". It was almost like a novelty record, you know. All the kids learned it; we all watched it on *Top of the Pops*, and we all memorized the lyrics because it was this fantastic novelty gimmick record that we all loved.

At school, we were all singing this song and learning the rhymes, but we weren't paying attention to "the Hip the Hop"; there was nothing in it that connected us to that

James McNally ▶ Rapper's Delight was an absolutely massive hit, almost like a dance record with rapping on it, rather than being understood as part of a culture originating from New York. I think people simply saw it as more of a novelty dance record, essentially.

Rapper's Delight was released at a particularly prolific and eclectic time for English music. Between the late 1970s and early 1980s, the London music scene was in constant expansion and evolution. Punk, New Wave and Disco were transforming the scene and new technologies were irreversibly transforming the way music was produced, especially when artists began experimenting with synthesisers and samplers.

The way music was consumed was also about to undergo a revolution. Funk, Rare Grooves and Reggae were the most popular genres among Black people.

Fraggle ▶ London back then had different musical genres which made it a unique place more than any other country in the world. So, if you take the decade of the 80s going up to 89 and so forth, you had different genres or different identities going on at the same time: you'd have Rastafarians, Skinheads, Punk rockers, New Romantics, people into Pop, etc. If I transported you back to that time, we could be standing on a street corner, and you would know straight away what musical genres an individual would be involved in or what he'd listen to.

Simon Reynolds ▶ Black music, technology, and the influence of Bowie/Roxy Music were the primary elements that defined the British music scene in the 1980s. It was a dynamic period, with an abundance of exceptional Black music originating from Jamaica, America, and Africa. Simultaneously, technology became more accessible, leading to a surge of innovative ideas.

Out of this creative explosion emerged various musical genres, such as Synth Pop, featuring artists like Soft Cell, Human League, Depeche Mode, Visage, Eurhythmics, and the New Romantic movement. While in America, Disco supposedly faded, in the UK, it continued to thrive. Disco and club music remained extremely popular, giving rise to the Jazz Funk scene. In the southern regions of England, including London and surrounding counties like Essex and Middlesex, people would attend all-day events, somewhat resembling legal raves. These gatherings took place in rented venues and ballrooms, where attendees would dance from morning till late into the night to the sounds of Jazz Funk. Weekenders that spanned the entire weekend were also a significant part of this culture, attracting thousands of young, multiracial participants who engaged in acrobatic dance moves. Renowned DJs were a fixture at these events, although they didn't mix tracks in the way that DJing would later become. Nevertheless, they attained cult status.

The British music scene of the '80s encompassed a wide range of subcultures, including the romantic Reggae scene known as Lovers Rock and the Roots scene. The Two Tone and Ska scene, which featured multiracial bands playing fast dance music, also made a mark. This genre had a strong retro vibe, with people often dressing in 1960s fashion.

The era was characterized by the simultaneous emergence of various Black music genres, including Dub, Disco, Funk, the early stages of Electro, and even African music represented by artists like Fela Kuti.

The third major driving force was the evolution of technology. Synthesizers became more affordable, compact, and portable. Previously, they were large and expensive machines only accessible to the affluent. Additionally, the availability of good drum machines and sequencers allowed for creating patterns, repeating them, and looping them. This led to the development of an electronic sound that was highly danceable due to its consistent rhythm.

Finally, the influence of artists like David Bowie and Roxy Music cannot be understated. For instance, Duran Duran's sound in the 1980s echoed the commercial sound of Roxy Music. Roxy Music had initially experimented with avant-garde music in the 1970s but shifted toward a more commercial sound when they regrouped in the late '70s. Their aim was to break into the American market and settle their debts with their record label. Other groups drew inspiration not only from Bowie's music but also from his distinctive look, fashion, and overall artistic approach.

Greg Wilson ▶ I mean basically from a UK perspective dance music started in the 60s with Motown, Stacks Atlantic, and the type of music that the mods would dance. It was huge. And people in this country had this obsession with Black music, it went back in the 50's with the discovery of Rhythm and Blues and the Blues. I'm part of that lineage, I would read magazines like Blues & Soul to get the information. It was really a special scene. It was underground obviously, a lot of these tracks crossed over to the mainstream eventually. The mid-seventies onwards, which is the time I started, was the Disco era. And Disco to us was basically the music playing in clubs and discotheques which was soul and funk, it wasn't a specific genre, it was still very much Black music.

MC Duke ▶ Reggae was a massive influence. It became a unifying force for Black people, bringing together individuals of African descent across all areas of London.

Norman Jay ▶ To me the '80s were an amazing time with music, the best decade ever as far as Black music. And this happened in those 10 years, Boogie, Disco, Electro, Hip Hop, Rare Grooves, RnB, Soulful House, Acid House and it all ended up in raves. These 10 years were the most creative time for music. Other than Disco, none of them were there before.[1]

With *Rapper's Delight*, the face of British Pop culture changed radically. With its fifteen minutes and thirty-six seconds of pure fun, with a profusion of wordplay, silly jokes

[1] Norman Jay, *Mister Good Times*, Dialogue, 2020, p. 270.

and memorable slang expressions that were easy to remember and repeat, that song with three MCs rhyming on the beat was warmly welcomed by the large Caribbean community due to the tradition of *Toasting*, the art of improvising bars on a beat, typical of the Reggae scene. For the young English people of that time, *Rapper's Delight* was considered a *novelty record*, because it did not provide any indication of the complexity of the movement that was vibrating in the streets of the Bronx. It would have taken more time, and the release of other records, music videos, books and movies, before that could happen. Hip Hop culture spread through several parallel channels, including pirate radios and cassette tapes mailed to friends, relatives and acquaintances, as well as 12-inch records imported from independent record labels.

New York City Rap Tour and Buffalo Gals

Two episodes in particular contributed to the understanding of Hip Hop as a parallel expression of different art forms: the 1982 *New York City Rap Tour* and the release of *Buffalo Gals* video by Malcolm McLaren. In November 1982, Fab Five Freddy and Kool Lady Blue, in collaboration with the radio station *Europe 1*, the retail chain FNAC and the French record labels *Celluloid* and *Disc 'AZ*, organised the *New York City Rap Tour*, the first-ever tour of all elements of Hip Hop culture outside the United States. The included artists represented the best DJs, breakers and writers of the time: Afrika Bambaataa, GrandMixer D.ST. & The Infinity Rappers, Rock Steady Crew, Futura 2000, Dondi, Phase 2, Rammellzee and the double-dutch jump-rope team The Fantastic Four. Although the audience turnout for the London show was disappointing, that event was seminal for the few who had the opportunity to attend, even if they weren't fully able to grasp what they were experiencing, at least not yet.

Fab Five Freddy ▶ In November of 1982, the plans were put in motion for the first Hip Hop tour in Europe, the New York City Rap Tour. About twenty of us – the Rock Steady Crew, Afrika Bambaataa, GrandMixer D.St and the Infinity MCs, PHASE 2, RAMMELLZEE, DONDI, and the Double Dutch Girls, went on a two-week tour of France, with one show in London.

Futura ▶ And in every town a backdrop was painted and tagged by DONDI and me, and the rest of you guys would cop a tag here and there, giving it the feel of a wall in some New York hood.[2]

Alex Mac ▶ In November '82, we showed up at Victoria, at a place called The Venue. It was a really peculiar event: there were some guys in the back doing something with records, and this strange group of girls appeared with skipping ropes. Then there were guys doing gymnastics to music on stage, others singing and rapping into microphones, and some were painting on canvases. It was called the New York City Rap Tour. It completely blew my mind because it was all so new, and I couldn't quite figure out what I was witnessing.

Janette Beckman's photographs are the only visual testimony of that event. When she found out about the *New York City*

[2] You can read the full interview with Futura here: https://artinthestreets. org/text/futura-talks-with-fab-5-freddy.

Poster for the
New York City
Rap Tour, 1982

Rap Tour, she asked the editor of the weekly *Melody Maker* magazine if she could photograph that show: "I actually had to beg them to let me go". Beckman had spent the period between 1977 and 1983 photographing Punk bands but "Punk was declining and here comes this new and exciting music. Before meeting Dondi, Lee and Futura, I had never seen anyone tagging. I captured amazing shots of Bambaataa and D.St. on the turntables and b- boy stances. I had a feeling that Hip Hop was going to be the next creative wave".[3]

[3] Read the full article here: https://www.npr.org/2022/11/26/1137418347/new-york-city-rap-tour.

A few days later, on November 19, 1982, the music TV show *The Tube* introduced the Scratch techniques and the foundations of Breaking to the British audience for the first time.

The occasion was the release of the single *Buffalo Gals* by Malcolm McLaren, a controversial character and former manager of the Sex Pistols, Bow Wow Wow and Adam and the Ants. However, he deserves credit for introducing the four elements of Hip Hop through the music video of that song. *Buffalo Gals* entered the top ten of the British pop chart in December 1982.

McLaren encountered Hip Hop culture while he was in Manhattan in the summer of 1981, when around that time he was looking for a support group for his artist Bow Wow Wow. Accompanied by the director Michael Holman, he found himself immersed in an Afrika Bambaataa block party in the Bronx. McLaren was deeply impressed by what he had seen and heard that night and decided to incorporate that style in his debut album, *Duck Rock*, and teamed up with the best British producer: Trevor Horn. To produce it, they took the recording studio on a sort of international tour, absorbing different musical styles and combining them in an original way.

In the BBC documentary *Beat This: A Hip Hop History*, directed by Dick Fontaine, Malcolm McLaren talks about that party in August 1981.

Malcolm McLaren ▶ I was working with a group called Bow Wow Wow and I was over there because they were signed to RCA Records and I was looking to put them on in a hall in Manhattan somewhere. The terrible thing was that I was really stuck for a responsible and exciting

Cover of the single *Buffalo Gals* by Malcolm McLaren, 1982

opening act. And there was nothing happening in New York at all and a friend of mine introduced me to a guy who I met on the street somewhere down on 5th Avenue who told me about an incredible scene that was happening not in Manhattan but in the suburb known as the South Bronx.

He said if I liked I could come down on a Saturday night where they were holding a big party and see something that couldn't possibly have ever existed in England. I decided to pitch up with him on Saturday night. Upon arriving at the party – unbeknown to me, I thought it was going to be inside a house but it was actually outside in the open, in a wasteland surrounded by these huge fired-out condominiums – there in the midst of it was about a thousand kids. I was very worried, being the only white guy there and the cab driver had given me the signal that I should put my dollars in my socks.

Nevertheless I escorted myself across the road with this

guy and made my way through the crowd, pushing and shoving until I got to where the music was coming from in front of these two decks and shook hands with this huge fat guy who later became known to me as Afrika Bambaataa. I witnessed various young kids popping in and out among the decks and messing with the records. It was extraordinary. As far as I could see the sound coming out was totally inarticulate, a load of rough noises, noises that sounded a little like a guitar but sort of like a concrete chisel sound, right? And I realised the sound came from the way they were messing around with their hands on the decks, moving records backwards and forwards, moving back and forth between the two.

In fact, it was making music out of other people's music. As time went on – and I stuck around for an hour or so – the crowd were extremely volatile and at times jumping into pitched battles. At one point or another, the crowd would move to the sides and a group of kids would start freaking out, doing incredible, gymnastic dancing.

The album cover of *Duck Rock* depicts a customised boombox with a pair of buffalo horns, while the cover of *Buffalo Gals* highlights the SL1200 Technics turntables, a model that had become ingrained in the very DNA of Hip Hop.

The visual fragments McLaren included in just over three minutes for the *Buffalo Gals* video created enough shock to ignite a youth movement in the United Kingdom and seemed deliberately crafted to promote the album. It was the first Hip Hop media product ever released on both sides of the Atlantic that combined all the expressive Hip Hop forms.

That record opened a glimpse into the reality of the

American cities. Moreover, the fast-paced editing of its videoclip, the quick body contortions, the colours of spray cans invading space and the gleaming chrome of technology made it even more fascinating. From that point forward, it's safe to say that youth culture in the UK underwent a profound transformation that would leave a lasting impact.

James MacNally ▶ Only a small group of people really got to see the New York City Rap Tour, so I don't think it had that big impact but almost immediately after that you got Buffalo Girls by Malcolm McLaren which, if you look at that video, got all the elements of Hip Hop in it. That was really a kind of a benchmark moment in unfolding it all.

Greg Wilson ▶ Before *Buffalo Gals* we were more or less completely unaware of Hip Hop (at least with regards to three of its four elements). We already knew about Rap of course, which had first made its mark in 1979 when The Sugarhill Gang scored a worldwide success with *Rappers Delight*, but the style had been dismissed by the British media as a novelty although perceptions had begun to change following the August '82 release of Grandmaster Flash & The Furious Five's street epic *The Message*. Scratching was still an abstract concept as far as British DJs were concerned; graffiti, as we then understood it, was hardly considered art, and we knew nothing whatsoever of Breakdancing.

Rodney P ▶ We knew what Hip Hop sounded like, but we didn't know what it looked like. In that video, we got to see Popping and Breakdancing for the first time; kids putting lino on the pavement, the graffiti writers and the DJs. All the elements were there. When that came out, it was as if the world had been spun on his head. Before rap took off in England it was all about the Breakdancing and Body Popping and that was introduced in England by Malcolm McLaren.

Greg Wilson ▶ I got a copy of the video on promo when I visited the same record company in London. It hadn't even been shown on TV yet, but they gave me a VHS copy. I took it with me and played it in a club. I decided that at one o'clock, I would play the video. It was the first time; no one had seen people spinning on their heads. It was just bizarre. That night, it was as if Martians had landed; people couldn't have been more surprised by what they witnessed on the screen. The crowd went as quiet as mice; what they were seeing had instantly changed their world. There was no point in going back to music after that video; people just wanted to see it again and again. It was as if there was no turning back from that.

Alex Mac ▶ Everyone began discussing the video and the incredible feats these kids were performing: one guy was spinning records, another was painting, and it all felt so refreshing, like a new form of music. For many, including myself, this marked the beginning of a journey into something we could explore, whether it was music, dance, art, or rapping on the microphone or whatever you were gonna do.

Bunny Bread ▶ Now, if it weren't for that video, I don't know when we would have fully grasped Hip Hop culture.

A lot of people watched that video, and then we'd go to school to meet our friends and say, "Did you see that video on *Top of the Pops*?". We saw it all as a complete package, you know, it's all in this one component. We realized that there's something for all of us, whether it's becoming a DJ, a graffiti writer, an MC, or a b-boy. There's something there for everybody.

DJ Pogo ▶ When they show you on *Top of the Pops* like a prime-time evening show then everybody is trying to do that. That was the show that everybody was watching religiously every Thursday night. After that video London understood what Hip Hop really was.

Greg Wilson ▶ As with Punk, Malcolm McLaren could clearly understand Hip Hop's role as a force for social change, for when all's said and done, these two major youth movements represent opposite sides of the same coin. Both Punk and Hip Hop made a lasting impact on popular culture in the UK and McLaren's role was absolutely crucial in each case.

It was as if that video had opened *Pandora's Box*, and all the street science from the Bronx poured onto British soil. Those young people not only had discovered new street practices, now they could observe and emulate them. In that video, there was everything: Rap and Scratch music, colourful graffiti and, of course, the most astonishing dance style, Breaking. This also included an unimaginable move at that time: there was a dancer rotating his entire body upside down, spinning on his head! If the news had broadcasted scenes of a hypothetical Martian landing, probably those young people would have been less astonished! Of course, London didn't turn into the Bronx! It was a sudden, unexpected novelty, but that offered opportunities to everyone regardless of their individual artistic inclinations. It would take months of total immersion in the four elements of Hip Hop, but that was the moment when the movement began to captivate more and more boys and girls.

Greg Wilson ▶ It wasn't an overnight change, how could it be when the full implications of what had appeared, as if by magic before our eyes, would take months to fully sink in, but change gradually came. It was a full-frontal introduction, it was all there, rapping and scratching, colourful graffiti pieces and, of course, the most amazing of dance styles which we'd come to know as breaking. The big thing was, the break dancing, that opened everything up and that brought everyone together, including a lot of the young white kids at the time who had never been in contact with Black culture, or even met Black people. It was a very unifying force absolutely.

Alex Mac ▶ Collectively, we formed small crews and began experimenting in local parks, subways, and other locations, trying to figure out how to do it. In those days, there weren't any manuals, and there weren't films like *Style Wars* or *Wild Style*, and *Subway Art* hadn't been published yet. These resources didn't exist, and nobody really knew what the hell to do, so we were basically doing it all wrong, learning through trial and error rather than having any reference material.

Skam One ▶ We didn't know how to do it, so we started approaching things differently, just figuring stuff out for ourselves, and it evolved in its own unique way.

Rodney P ▶ I mean places like Battersea Park were quite localized. Every area had its own spot. For us South London kids, Battersea Park was where we would gather, set up small stages, host shows, and have sound systems, allowing us to perform and hone our skills. This is where we learned the trade in many ways.

Remedee ▶ Around London, there were various pockets of people diving into Hip Hop. You had North London, South London (considered the 'home of Hip Hop'), East London, and so on. In these areas, you'd find different crews, MCs, and breakers each doing their own thing in their respective neighborhoods.

After *Buffalo Gals*, Breaking and graffiti started gaining progressively more popularity becoming the chosen weapons to rebel and subvert the hierarchies of urban spaces and the youth policies of the Callaghan's government first, and Thatcher's later.

Just like in the United States, although to a significantly different extent, the working-class neighbourhoods of British cities had experienced severe budget cuts that intensified during the transition from the 1970s to the 1980s. Margaret Thatcher's neoliberal administration privatised the gas, steel, and telecommunication industries, resulting in a steep rise in unemployment rate and cuts to funding for the arts, recreational activities and youth centres. This was the reality in which British Hip Hop culture emerged. The pioneers of the scene were precisely those young people who were most affected by those policies.

James McNally ▶ In the 1970s up until the early '80s, a huge deindustrialization process was going on, so the economy was changing...

Alex Mac ▶ We had the Three-Day Week where basically people didn't work for 4 of the 7 days, electricity was turned off after 5 o'clock, so it was quite a bleak time for people. things had gone into absolute decline, housing had gone into decline, there wasn't investment, and unemployment was starting to rise. So in '79 the voting public decided to have a change and voted in what everybody knows as the Tory government. Moving into the 80's, you had the Thatcher government coming in and they had to make some very harsh and incredibly unpopular decisions; a lot of governmental spending was cut back and a lot of things got impacted like youth programs, like investments in the arts and crafts and things like that.

MC Mello ▶ In the 80s, youth clubs in our neighborhoods were being closed down, poverty was on the rise, people didn't have money, and job opportunities were scarce. But worst of all, there was a sense among us youngsters that nobody cared about us, that no one cared about us.

Bunny Bread ▶ In 1980, Margaret Thatcher came to power, and for the youth, especially young Black kids, it was not a great time. Politically and socially, things like the Sus law started to emerge. If you were young, male, and Black, you could be stopped by the police, and they

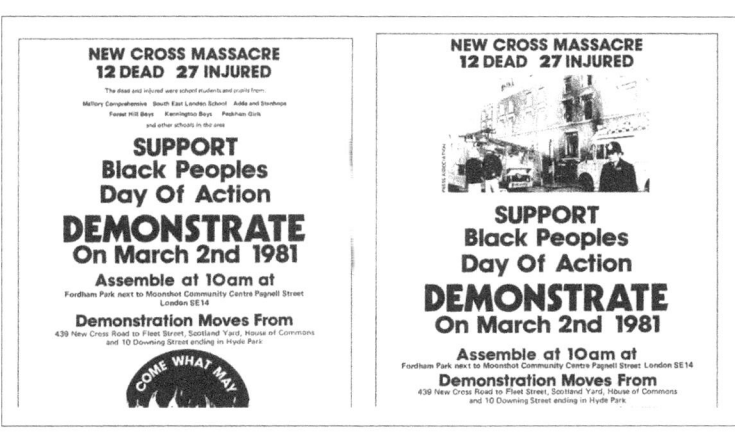

Poster for the Black Day of Action, 1981

would say, "We're going to search you", and, if necessary, "we're going to put you in the back of the van, and if need be, we'll take you down to the police station for a couple of hours", all without any apparent reason.

DJ Devastate ▶ The law was designed to target and search young Black men, which contributed to a strong sense of distrust among many young Black men towards the police.

In 1981, the Black population of London, increasingly under siege, revolted. The death of thirteen Black teenagers, which occurred in January due to a fire that broke out during a house party at 439 New Cross Road in South West London, had set the stage for a day of protest called the *Black People's Day of Action*. This incident is crucial to understanding the dynamics of racism in the UK: violence, police abuse, neglect by the state, but at the same time, it also tells of the story of the resistance of the Black community. There were reports of Molotov cocktails being thrown by sympathisers of the National Front, but the hasty judicial investigation ended with no concrete outcome. Given the deafening silence of the government and media and the authorities' lack of interest, on March 2nd, a diverse crowd marched protesting from the site of the tragedy to the centre of London, despite repeated attempts by the police to stop the march.

During the journey, the participants sang *Thirteen Dead (Nothing Said)* by the Reggae musician Johnny Osbourne to denounce the disregard for Black lives in England. Other artists told the story of that tragedy through Reggae songs and poems like *13 Dead* by Benjamin Zephaniah, Linton Kwesi Johnson's *New Cross Massakah* and UB40's *Don't Let It Pass You By*, while Menelik Shabazz's documentary *Blood Ah Go Run* is a testimony to the response of the Black community. The title itself, *Blood Ah Go Run If Justice No Come*, recalls a slogan from the March 2nd protest announcing the wave of urban riots. In April of the same year, the London police launched *Operation Swamp 81* to tackle a surge in crime in the city. During their attempt to intervene in the case of a young man's injury, the officers found themselves facing a crowd that thought the young man, Michael Bailey, was under arrest.

Tensions skyrocketed. While they were taking him away, the first riots broke out because rumours were circulating that the young man had died in the hospital, and some claimed that he had been killed by an officer.

Immediately after, a van was searched and the driver stopped. This incident proved to be the final straw. At five o'clock in the afternoon on Saturday, April 11th, Brixton turned into a battlefield and the fierce uprising lasted for two days. The *Time* described that day of clashes *Black Saturday*,

with 280 injured among the police and 45 among the pro-
testers. More than a hundred cars were set on fire, including
56 police vehicles, at least 150 buildings were damaged and
about thirty of them burned down. In the end, there were 82
arrests. The London riots were the spark that ignited riots in
other cities. Between July 3rd and 11th, 1981, riots erupted
in Handsworth (Birmingham), Southall (London), Toxteth
(Liverpool), Hyson Green (Nottingham), Moss Side (Manchester) and Chapeltown (Leeds). The discontent against
racism and unemployment also erupted in Southampton, Hal-
ifax, Bedford, Gloucester, Wolverhampton, Coventry, Bristol
and Edinburgh, all places marked by racial discrimination
and poverty. In his autobiography, *The Life and Rhymes of
Benjamin Zephaniah* (2018) the dub poet Zephaniah argues
that those riots should be understood as uprisings motivated
by decades of humiliation and mistreatment at the hands of
the police. Paul Gilroy refers to them as *tumultuous protests*,
while Linton Kwesi Johnson titled one of his songs *Great
Insohreckshan*, included in his famous album *Making History*.
In 2020 a documentary in three episodes titled *Uprising* and
directed by Steve McQueen and James Rogan was released
by the BBC. It serves as a real exploration of racism in Great
Britain, specifically revisiting the events of 1981, including
the *New Cross Fire*, the *Black People's Day of Actio*n and the
Brixton riots.

During those years, unemployment in neighbourhoods
like Brixton stood around 13%, but ethnic minorities experienced it at a rate of 25.4%. Among young Black people
it reached 55%. By refusing to invest in the regeneration
of the poorest urban areas, Thatcher argued that "money can't buy trust and racial harmony". The tensions that
had caused those riots were still burning, and the level of

control had increased, generating a growing frustration over the progressive marginalisation of Black neighbourhoods. Among the tools adopted there were the *Sus Laws*: *Sus* was the abbreviation for *suspicious person*, a definition so vague it left room for police interpretation, authorising them to stop and arrest individuals based solely on mere suspicion. These laws were used entirely discretionary to exclude the presence of Black people from some areas, especially those frequented by wealthy white individuals.

The extremely high number of stops and arrests taking place in the city's West End, a tourist and business area, were a clear indication that this law was a weapon of repression and social control, not only towards the impoverished Black community affected by the recession, but also towards broader sectors of the urban youth proletariat. A true segregation wall divided the city into separate spaces, fueling controversies on the so-called race relations that dominated the media. Margaret Thatcher, after all, won the elections in 1979 becoming prime minister with a program aimed at strengthening the resources and powers of the police. Her government pursued a political agenda focused on law and order, which viewed Blacks as an inherent threat to the way of life of white England.

Jonzi D ▶ Being young and Black in England was a real challenge, and I would say that the children of that generation had to figure things out for ourselves. We had to come together as a community.

Dirty Harry ▶ The 70s in England were tough; there was a recession, and it was really difficult. We didn't have much, but we had each other, and that was important.

Music played a vital role in bringing us together during those times.

In 1983, *Street Sounds*, a London-based record label, launched a series of albums called *Electro*. These compilations included the most popular American Electro and Rap songs, featuring crews, DJs and MCs like Newcleus, Egyptian Lover, Cybotron, Captain Rock, Grandmaster Flash, RUN DMC and Mantronix. *Electro Funk* is a sub-genre that emerged in a specific historical period, the early 1980s, when electronic music influenced by The Kraftwerk intersected with Funk and Hip Hop music. In its original form, it was nothing but Black science fiction transported on to the dance floors of New York, Miami and Los Angeles. It was a fusion of video games, techno-pop, graffiti, spacesuits and cyborg Funk. With few exceptions, *Electro Funk* is characterised by the massive use of drum machines, funk synth basslines, reverb, echo and synthesiser effects. The term was not coined by a specific artist or in conjunction with the release of a particular record, but it began to be used because it appeared in tracks like *On a Journey (I Sing the Funk Electric)* by Electrik Funk and *Electrophonic Phunk* by Shock. The circle was closed in May 1982 with the release of *Planet Rock* by Bambaataa & The Soulsonic Force. Never before Rap music had been tied to such fast and electronic rhythms. The Rap songs released in these compilations included both classics of the old school and tracks from artists of the golden age, offering the British audience a sort of *best-of* that narrated the evolution of the genre throughout that decade. We are talking about artists who received extensive coverage in the UK years before signing any type of contract for a major label. The *Street Sounds* productions were more than just albums: they were, in fact, a direct channel of communication between the audiences on both coasts of the Atlantic.

The songs featured in those compilations helped to better introduce the leading figures from the United States, quickly becoming the soundtrack of the first generation of British Hip Hoppers. And they were also affordable for everyone: in the early 1980s, in fact, a 12-inch single cost about 2 pounds, 4 if it was an import. Those compilations contained eight singles and cost less than 5 pounds. The strong commercial feedback ensured its distribution to local retailers, which also allowed suburban and provincial kids to purchase the records of their favourite artists.

This was the beginning of a path of awareness that permeated in the social fabric devastated by Thatcher's policies.

As Blues & Soul writer Damon Rochefort explained in an article called *Khan's Kingdom* (April '84), Street Sounds "totally revolutionised the entire dance music industry by making available, at a more-than reasonable price, a remarkable selection of the very latest dance hits within the financial reach of the country's younger end of the dance music market".

Greg Wilson ▶ These compilations were released by Morgan Khan on his Streets Sounds label starting in October 1983. He would curate 7 or 8 tracks on each album, and Herbie from Mastermind was in charge of the mixing.

Rodney P ▶ At the time, the Street Sounds albums were life-changing for us. We would eagerly await their release for weeks. They featured the most popular Hip Hop tunes of the time, and many of them were electro tracks.

Morgan Khan ▶ In 1983 we released the first compilation titled *Electro*. It became instantly very popular. Its popularity didn't stem only from the songs that were featured, what we did was intercepting a mood, a state of mind.

Like its American counterpart, the London scene developed primarily through the exchange of cassette tapes containing recordings of the performances of the best MCs from the United States. Those who had friends or family in New York or were lucky enough to visit, became a sort of gatekeepers, the preachers of that new *gospel*. Anyone who owned the cassette tapes was a member of a sort of secret society, invisible to those who did not know the access codes. Those tapes passed from hand to hand, also because the boxes had a minimal size, they could fit into a pocket and circulated easily. As convenient as they were, they were also fragile: the tapes would deteriorate quickly and every play inevitably corrupted the sound quality.

Having such a small product in your hands was considered almost magical. Discovering the name of the various crews by deciphering the densely handwritten tracklist was a way to better understand what was happening in the scene, but the most exhilarating moment came during the listening experience. Young people would spend hours and hours in their bedrooms repeatedly imitating the flow of the MCs, eagerly anticipating the opportunity to try it out on the streets with their friends.

MC Duke ▶ In the beginning, it was like niche music, confined to a small group of us because we were the ones with the tapes. If you didn't have them, you wouldn't hear the music, and that's how the Hip Hop community grew in London.

Greg Wilson ▶ If you were an average person, you might not even be aware that these new cultures existed. However, if you stumbled upon the right radio station or walked into the right record shop and got the right tape, you became connected and started to understand that this whole culture was happening.

POWER OF THE CASSETTE TAPES

When Dutch engineer Lou Ottens introduced the compact cassette tapes in 1963, no one could have imagined that it would revolutionise the world of music. Yet, by the 1970s, that small medium had transformed into a revolutionary and sub-versive technology. Its importance was linked to portability and affordability, but above all to ease of recording and distribution. On one hand, it allowed many musicians to work outside the expensive recording studios, leading to the development of new musical genres. On the other hand, it provided listeners with the ability to record songs and radio shows without spending money on purchasing records. The liberating effect of the cassette tapes began to spread in the 1970s with Punk, the first Rap and later with post-Punk and Electronic music. These genres, as we know them today, would not exist in these forms without cassette tapes.

In New York, the first aspiring beatmakers and MCs began their career producing breakbeat loops. For example, as Jeff Chang writes in his book *Can't Stop Won't Stop*, in 1973 DJ Kool Herc used two copies of the same record to create a loop from a song, "extending a five-second break into five minutes of fire". This technique, implemented with a double cassette deck, allowed producers to understand how to create suitable beats to rhyme over.

Even the parties of the early Hip Hop pioneers like Kurtis Blow, Grandmaster Flash, Afrika Bambaataa and Kool Herc himself were recorded on cassette tapes and spread throughout the community as *party tapes*. These tapes began to circulate even beyond national borders, bringing the music of the South Bronx to the world. Only those who owned them, as recalled by MC Duke, had the keys to access that still totally underground movement.

Grandmaster Flash would give his tapes to taxi drivers to play for their customers, or he would charge a high price to richest fans, customising them by shouting the buyer's name during his DJ sets. In an interview with MTV in 2007, Flash said he used to earn about two thousand dollars a month from the tapes. During its early years, Rap music existed exclusively as live performance: parties organised in community centres or jams in public parks. Only in 1979 the first vinyl record was released, but for much of the decade, it was those tapes encapsulated within two pieces of plastic that travelled everywhere, turning young artists into cult figures and greatly enhancing Rap's ability to attract a younger audience. Without those tapes, those parties would have been remembered only in the memories of those who attended them, severely limiting their global diffusion.

With the arrival of the *Walkman*, music became portable, with the emergence of the *boombox* or *ghetto blaster*, listening became collective, further promoting the spread of the tapes. They were like small and harmless weapons against the overwhelming dominance of multinational record companies. Once it became possible to move around the city with one's own music, a sonic revolution was literally in the hands of anyone, regardless of race, gender or social class.

In the mid-1980s, in Camden market in London, thousands and thousands of bootleg tapes of concerts and mixed compilations with the major US and British hits were sold.

Every weekend Camden was the destination for thousands of music enthusiasts in search of the latest releases. Some sellers would draw illustrations or tags on the brightly coloured cardboards to make them easily identifiable. Inside, they would list the names of the artists and the song titles, which were very valuable information at the time. Big Al, one of the most well-known tapes dealers in the scene, disappeared from the business after a raid by the Anti Piracy Unit in 1987, during which "*4605 tapes with an estimated value of over £ 20,000*" were seized, according to a report by *Music Week*.

Just like cassette tapes, videotapes were an important vector in the evolution of Hip Hop culture. Although it is a lesser-known aspect, the recording of videos, clips of television programs and films on VHS tapes played a significant role.

At the beginning of the 1980s, technological advancement made it easier for people to purchase video recorders, which became prominent fixtures in households. With these devices you could watch and rewatch several times videos and music video clips, but most importantly, record and then study the fashion, movements, speech and technique of using sprays and turntables at your own convenience.

Also in 1983, the film *Wild Style* by Charlie Ahearn was released in England, and subsequently the *Style Wars* documentary by Henry Chalfant and Tony Silvers. These two milestones became pivotal in providing a comprehensive understanding of American Hip Hop culture and subsequently raising awareness among young English people to create their own homegrown local scene. The scenario of *Wild Style* is the South Bronx in its poorest and most desperate version. The protagonists are the legends of writing, Lee Quinones and Lady Pink. Then there are Fab Five Freddy, the Rock Steady Crew showcasing their best dance moves, DJs like Grandmaster Flash and MCs like the Cold Crush Brothers, Kool Moe Dee, Busy Bee Starski, and many other pioneers of the old school scene in all their swagger.

Wild Style is a very precious document because it represents a culture that no one else knew beyond the five boroughs of NYC. This is how Fab Five Freddy comments: "One day I saw a group of b-boys performing in a public square, I decided to watch their show. At first, I was amazed that they knew what Breaking was in general, but after a few minutes, I realised they were imitating the moves of the Rock Steady Crew, right like in the film. In that moment I understood how Wild Style was helping to spread Hip Hop around the world".

Style Wars is instead a documentary on Writing filmed in the 1980s, a golden age of youthful creativity set against the backdrop of a New York in full economic crisis. Style Wars highlights how the dilapidated subway system can turn into an outdoors playground, a battleground and an immense travelling canvas that writers used to leave their own mark. A fundamental element that unites the two films is the concept of style, a style that had little to do with fashion, but rather with the visceral need to find specific skills and identity. It was about developing unique and original expressive methods to make oneself heard, despite the marginalisation in which the Black areas had sunk. Both films depict the poorest neighbourhoods as multicultural and multiracial spaces, emphasising the young age of the scene's protagonists.

Simon Reynolds ▶ When the films came over, things changed.

James McNally ▶ Wild Style came out here in September 1983 and it was distributed through the ICA which is the Institute of Contemporary Arts. For the kids who actually sought it out, it was an hour and a half of this exciting stuff that they had seen only for 3 minutes on Malcolm McLaren's video on TV. No one really had a hold of what the kind of iconography that went with Hip Hop was. What Wild Style did in London was to give us a sense of what was going on and how things kind of fitted together. I think the amphitheatre scene at the end is the template of how they saw it was meant to be done for a whole generation of people involved in Hip Hop in London.

MC Mello ▶ We witnessed authenticity in everything, from the way the DJs and rappers performed to the venues they selected, the lighting, and the atmosphere. Watching *Breaking*, listening to the lyrics, and soaking in the vibes had a profound impact on the young Hip Hop enthusiasts of that era. It was absolutely mind-blowing. It became a way of life – you'd wake up, eat, and breathe *Wild Style*, trying to emulate everything you saw in the movie.

Pride ▶ I came across a magazine and noticed the graffiti tag "Wild Style", and I was immediately intrigued. I had no idea what "Wild Style" meant, but the marker pen inscription in a bold and eccentric style piqued my curiosity. The article was promoting a film that was being screened at the I.C.A (Institute of Contemporary

Poster for the screening of Wild Style at the ICA, September 1983

Arts). It mentioned Fab Five Freddy and a sound system from my area, Mastermind, being part of the event, and it completely blew my mind. I had no prior knowledge that this culture existed in such a vibrant way. I saw people my age and even younger, all in a diverse urban setting, particularly young Black individuals showcasing their extraordinary creativity. What struck me were the similarities between the sound systems and club culture, which resonated with my own experiences. After the film screening, another guy approached me and asked, "Hey, do you want to go to Covent Garden?" I was initially unsure why I should go there at that moment, but he explained that it was a popular hangout spot where people were practicing breakdancing. Since I didn't know much about the culture, I decided to go and check it out. That night, I received an introduction to this world from both a New York City perspective and a UK perspective, and it all became very real to me.

Pirate radios also played a fundamental role in spreading Hip Hop music; they were like social networks, long before Facebook and Instagram. In the 1980s and into the early 1990s, illegal radio stations dominated the airwaves in England, providing a vital outlet for street expressions that were not represented in mainstream culture. The images associated with them is reminiscent of the early offshore broadcasting studios on ships outside territorial boundaries in the 1960s, but pirate radios experienced a sort of revival twenty years later, thanks to the technology of that time. During those years, the rooftops of council houses in the South and East of London were filled with antennas illegally installed to broadcast their shows.

The taller and more dangerous buildings were the most suitable because they complicated police operations. All they needed were keys, easily obtained from a tenant, and an affordable transmitter. These radios provided a platform of visibility for all those artists who would never appear on the playlists of commercial radio stations, and quickly became a tool for discovering new musical trends within Black communities. Dread Broadcasting Corporation (DBC), Radio Invicta, Kiss FM, London Weekend Radio (LWR), and Horizon were among the first pirate radio stations in the United Kingdom dedicated to Soul, Funk, Jazz, Reggae, and Hip Hop music.

Simon Reynolds ▶ The original pirate radio stations emerged in the 1960s, and they were truly "pirate" in nature, operating from ships anchored just outside British territory or waters. They played 1960s pop music with an American-style presentation, filled with high energy, in stark contrast to the BBC's approach. BBC only allocated two hours of pop music on a channel called The Light Program, featuring middle-aged and somewhat dull music with a touch of rock and roll. Pirate radio stations filled the void and quickly gained millions of listeners. Many of the DJs from these pirate stations were later recruited by BBC for Radio 1, the prominent national legal pop station. As time passed, the number of pirate radio stations dwindled as they were declared illegal and forced to shut down.

At noon on March 28, 1964, aboard a ship off the coast of Essex, DJs Chris Moore and Simon Dee announced the start of broadcasting for a new radio station by transmitting a pre-recorded message: "This is Radio Caroline, your twenty-four-hour music station a day". The first song played was *Not Fade Away* by the Rolling Stones. The broadcast had begun for what would become one of the world's first pirate radios and certainly the most famous one, whose story inspired the renowned film *I Love Radio Rock,* released in 2009.

In 1964, in England there were the Beatles, the Moody Blues, the Who, the Rolling Stones, Eric Clapton's Yardbirds, and the Kinks. In the midst of this unique pop music scene, the airwaves were still dominated by the three BBC radio channels, which relegated that music only to a few hours per week and excluded groups from independent labels. The rigid taste and some complicated regulations of the state broadcaster made things even more complicated. But the law, in the United Kingdom as elsewhere, ended just a few kilometres away from the coast; beyond that limit, one was in international waters and free from the constraints of legislation. Radio Caroline didn't remain the only pirate radio station for long. In the following months, many others were born: Radio Atlanta, Swinging Radio England, Radio Scotland, Radio London, BBMS. The golden age didn't last long as the government put an end to those experiences with the Marine Offences Act, which came into effect on August 15, 1967. The law, still in force, "prohibits broadcasting from ships, off-shore structures and aircrafts in British territorial waters, or from ships and aircrafts registered in the United Kingdom wherever they may be".

Simon Reynolds ▶ Pirate radios made a resurgence in the early '80s, primarily due to the fact that there were music genres the BBC was reluctant to play, such as Reggae and later Hip Hop. There was a shortage of Black music for both Black and White listeners alike. Pirate radios had a broadcast range of around 5 to 10 miles, so if you could tune in, you felt connected to a community of people in your vicinity. These stations played music that hadn't been released yet or music you wouldn't hear elsewhere, introducing the latest and brand-new sounds. It was an exhilarating experience.

In the early 1980s, FM transmitters started becoming affordable to purchase. Modern transistors allowed for a range of up to forty miles with a simple antenna placed on any city building. Thanks to these radios, Soul, Reggae and Hip Hop lovers had the opportunity to listen to radio shows that could satisfy all their hunger for music.

All that was needed was a good quality cassette deck and a transmitter placed on a sufficiently high roof. Music, but not only, for example tips on parties and events, vital information to immerse oneself in the beloved scene and find the so-called *warehouse parties*, the next illegal underground event in some abandoned factory.

On Wednesday nights on the frequencies of *Radio Invicta*, you could listen to the DJs of *Mastermind Roadshow* cutting, scratching and mixing live. *Invicta* was the first radio station to broadcast a certain genre of Black music for Black people, one of the first to introduce stereo broadcasts and live shows from a set up placed at the event location. *Radio Invicta* set the guidelines for all the other radio stations that emerged shortly thereafter. *LWR (London Weekend Radio)*, for example, was initially conceived as a Rock and Pop radio but later switched to Soul and Dance music, introducing a groundbreaking Rap show hosted by Tim Westwood, which quickly became the bible for all London b-boys. The radio was known as "The Home of Hip Hop". At the time, it was said that Tim Westwood' show managed to bring the South Bronx to South London.

In the West London area, *Dread Broadcasting Corporation (DBC)*, founded by Daddy Lepke, instead offered a mix of Reggae, Soul, Calypso, Funk and Hip Hop music.

Mekka Dbc ▶ The DBC Rebel Radio, which stood for Dread Broadcasting Corporation, was a pioneering sound system. It was the first to establish connections with other sound systems and even function as a pirate radio station at all-day events. DBC played a wide range of music genres, from Blues and Jazz to Rap, Reggae, and even African music. Many individuals who started their careers in music, such as Neneh Cherry, were associated with the station. I believe her DJ name was DJ Neneh C. She later achieved significant success with hits like *Buffalo Stance*,

Flyer for the pirate radio station Dread Broadcasting Corporation

which topped the charts in the UK. Another DJ, Ms. P, went on to host the first Reggae show on BBC Radio 1, titled *Culture Rock*. DBC wasn't exclusively for the Black community; it aimed to provide music for everyone, but it also served as a media entity for the Black community.

In those same years, Kiss FM was also born, launched in 1985 by Gordon Mac, Tosca and George Power.

Gordon Mac ▶ I started working part-time as a DJ on JFM, a pirate radio station, for three days a week. I learned the ins and outs of pirate radio through my experiences there. However, in early 1985, they were shut down by a major raid from the Department of Trade and Industry, and all the other stations were also going off the air while chasing the possibility of obtaining a community radio station license, which never materialized.

One night, around 1984, while I was DJing at Kiss, George Power, who also worked at Kiss on Sunday nights, approached me with the idea of starting a pirate radio station. He had already secured an engineer for the project, and that's how it all began. After a year, I bought out the others involved, but I didn't have enough funds to run the station, so I ended up selling back 45% of the shares to some of our DJs at Kiss FM.

We borrowed our name and logo from an American radio station. I discovered Kiss FM in New York, where they played non-stop, extended mixes of various tracks and even remixed them on air. I was thrilled and thought, "That's exactly what I want". Our vision was to create a pirate radio station for Black music lovers that covered a broad spectrum of genres. I aimed to assemble the best DJs from every musical style, and our team of DJs quickly became well-known names.

In the early months of 1985, Horizon, JFM, LWR, and other stations were forced to go off the air. That's when we stepped in, filling the void in the marketplace. We operated our transmitter from the top of an unstable roof, which the police couldn't remove, allowing us to keep broadcasting. This gave us the momentum we needed, and more DJs wanted to join our station. By 1988, we had incorporated nearly every significant street sound and club night of the era into Kiss's programming, providing early exposure to some of the UK's most influential tastemakers.

Kiss FM was a perfect storm. When we started, our primary focus was nurturing the incredible music we loved. That's why we became known as 'The Voice of Young London.

Terry Farley ▶ Kiss was absolutely massive. On Saturdays we would walk up and down King's Road and Oxford Street, buying music and clothes, and every shop had Kiss on.[4]

Fresh Ski ▶ You may remember those radio stations like Invicta and LWR, where the DJs would spin the latest 12-inch records. It was all about tuning in late at night, adjusting your antenna just right, and often struggling with a shaky signal. You'd find yourself saying, "I can't hear it, what's that tune?" while desperately trying to tape it at the same time...

Linton Lee ▶ Hip Hop began to make its way in, and we started tuning in to pirate radio stations. People were eager to catch those sounds from across the pond in New York. Word started spreading, 'Have you heard this stuff, man?'

Dave VJ ▶ Invicta allowed us, as Mastermind, to showcase a kind of music that was unavailable elsewhere. The only place you could hear it was when we played it on the airwaves. People would record it and listen to those tapes all week until the next broadcast, eagerly waiting to create another tape.

Norman Jay ▶ You have to remember this is pre-internet days, pre-global networking days so new media was the coming of pirate radios – we could start pirate radios. Kiss

---

[4] https://daily.redbullmusicacademy.com/2017/06/london-warehouse-parties-oral-history.

Cover of the first English rap single, *London Bridge Is Falling Down*, 1983

was the all-important voice, it accurately reflected what was really going on in the streets.[5]

1983 marked a turning point. Bertram Johnson, known on the scene as a DJ Newtrament, released along with MCs Sir Drew and Monoman what is considered the first English Rap single, *London Bridge Is Falling Down*. Although it was a song that addressed the English reality, with its references to the *boys in blue* and explicit criticism of Thatcher's policies, the spoken delivery had a distinct American accent. This element would be a common feature of all the rap singles released in the first half of the 1980s. DJ Newtrament was also the founder of *Rock Box*, London's first Hip Hop sound system. The parties he organised became a means of spreading Hip Hop to an increasingly wider audience. At that time, that budding scene consisted of small crews, mostly unaware

[5] Lloyd Bradley, *Sounds Like London*, Serpent's Tail, London 2013, p. 326.

of what was happening in other areas of the city. That's why those early parties with sound systems represented precious moments of aggregation and sharing experiences.

Dizzi Heights ▶ Newtrament was an American guy who joined our group. He came all the way from America with Drew, and they were part of a younger crew. We welcomed him with open arms. While I might have been one of the first to sign with a major record label, the actual first Hip Hop record would have been *London Bridge* by my friend Newtrament.

James McNally ▶ Dizzi Height's record *Christmas Rapping* was ahead of its time in terms of Hip Hop awareness. It was essentially a rap record layered over a more generic dance music track. Newtrament was part of a crew that included Mono Man and Sir Drew, and they were associated with Krew, a comprehensive organization based in Ladbroke Grove. By 1983, they had dancers, graffiti artists, and individuals involved in every aspect of Hip Hop.

Sir Drew ▶ I saw Newtrament as our version of Malcolm McLaren. Just like McLaren, he went to NYC and drew inspiration from the culture while aiming to make some money. Newtrament came into the scene, learned how to DJ, and had a desire to create a record.

MC Mello ▶ Newtrament was also the individual behind the creation of Rock Box. He took the foundational elements of Reggae sound systems and established the first UK Hip Hop sound system. He, along with all the

Cover of *Christmas Rapping* by Dizzi Heights, 1982

MCs, DJs, b-boys, and graffiti writers who attended those parties, laid the groundwork for the birth of a local scene.

DJ Pogo ▶ With significant funds from a major deal, he sponsored illegal warehouse parties. He would frequently travel to New York and return with the latest records. He emulated everything happening in New York, whether it was a park jam or a warehouse event. His sound system was called Rox Box.

Fresh Ski ▶ Once people heard about Rock Box, it was only a matter of time before someone would break into a warehouse somewhere in West London to set up a Hip Hop event.

Norman Jay ▶ At that time there were a great deal of empty industrial buildings in London, in pre-development areas like Goods Way in King's Cross; where Westfields stands just north of the Shepherd Bush roundabout; Curtain road by Old Street, Tooley Street in between the southern ends of London and Tower Bridges; or what became the Olympic park, just south of Hackney Wick. To the resourceful soundmen, these disused offices and warehouses were dancehall waiting to happen.[6]

Terry Farley (DJ/Promoter, The Raid) ▶ The parties were in dilapidated, ex-industrial areas like the Docks, Hackney Road, Old Street and Curtain Road (which had a lot of warehouses because of the commercial rag trade) Lots Road in Chelsea and even places out in the suburbs, like Wembley. It was a reaction against the West End and the licence laws. People wanted to get away from the restrictions of the West End.[7]

James McNally ▶ In London during the 1970s and up to the early '80s, a significant deindustrialization process was unfolding. Many warehouses in London were closing down as shipping operations moved out to places like Essex. The economy was undergoing changes, with factories shutting their doors. During this unique period, there were numerous abandoned buildings due to these shifts. The big bang of international finance that characterized the 1980s had not yet arrived. It was a time filled with opportunities to break into these empty structures and throw parties.

---

[6] Ibidem.
[7] https://daily.redbullmusicacademy.com/2017/06/london-warehouse-parties-oral-history.

Bunny Bread ▶ I remember one incredible party that Newtrament organized in East London in a dark, hidden warehouse. It took us hours to locate it. Inside, it was pitch dark with only a few dim lights coming in from the streets. Newtrament had set up in the middle, under a camouflaged tent that covered his sound system. It looked quite extraordinary. He was in the center, playing underneath the tent, and we partied all night long to an eclectic mix of music, including Electro, Funk, James Brown, Sly and the Family Stone, The Meters, Cool and the Gang, and more. He played a wide range of obscure tracks, even early Hip Hop and Electro, featuring releases from Tommy Boy Records and Sugar Hill.

Fresh Ski ▶ Rock Box was a weird conglomerate of all sorts of madness; you had b-boys and rappers and strange punky-type of people, and vagabonds. It just looked mad, when you walked into Rock Box, you're like "what's going on?". There's two men snogging in the corner, there's these b-boys breakdancing here, there's someone cutting beats not on time on the decks, it was a crazy scene, but people loved it, and there was a real buzz about it.

James McNally ▶ You'd have kind of like high fashioned people, you'd have kind of ex Punks, you'd have kind of all sorts of people maybe like Rockabillies with their big quiffs and stuff, and soul boys and Hip Hop kids and then some Rastas, you know, there was... a kind of very much open affair for kind of just people who wanted to be part of a exciting, slightly edgy kind of music scene. It definitely wasn't just kind of your b-boys standing there in their b-boy stance.

ROCK BOX IN EFFECT.

SUN, 16, AUGUST.

AT "MEANWHILE GARDENS"

TIME; 12 PM - 6 PM

TUBE; WESTBORN PARK , BUSES; 27 31

PLUS → A SKATE BOARD COMPETITION FOR THE MOST RADICAL SKATERS

"THE OFFICIAL ROADBLOCK JAM"

YOUR GONNA GET YOURS !

NEUTRAMENT®
SIR DREW
D.J. KILA
NOISE®
FRESH SKI®
SHE ROCKERS®
AND
KREW

E... BUM RUSH... ITS FREE... FREE... FREE... BUM

Flyer for a Rock Box party

Jay Strongman ▶ The emphasis was on partying, and it wasn't about the décor or the light show. A damp dark room with one red light bulb, a booming sound system and a reputation was the prerequisite for success back then. It was risky and addictive.[8]

Bunny Bread ▶ What we loved about Newtrament was that he was relentless, he was playing this hard tough b-boy music all night long.

---

[8] https://daily.redbullmusicacademy.com/2017/06/london-warehouse-parties-oral-history.

West End

In 1984, Covent Garden, once an indoor fruit and vegetable market but later transformed into a popular tourist area in the heart of London, became the focal point for Hip Hop, giving the city's scene an impetus that had been lacking until then. Due to the still recent memory of the *Bloody Saturday* incident and the ongoing criminalization of Black youth, reclaiming a relatively safe place, in the heart of the city where they could engage in Hip Hop practices, was considered a significant achievement and had contributed to change social mobility. Covent Garden, in fact, was accessible from all over London, serving as a neutral ground for young people coming from different areas and cities, and it was also the only space where *busking* (asking for money after the performances) was legal. This, in fact, was the main reason that led many b-boys and writers to choose that place as a gathering spot and performance venue. They were trying to make money legally, showing off their creative skills. Words of mouth did the rest, quickly transforming Covent Garden into the *Mecca* of London's Hip Hop scene, as stated by Rodney P of the London Posse, one of the key figures of those years.

By reading the posts on the Facebook page of the *London Hip Hop Fraternity* group, it's easy to understand how that place became a magnet of creativity and style, which proved crucial not only for the consolidation of the scene, but also for its evolution into something else.

Greg Wilson ▶ Much of this was rooted in the idea that Black individuals wanted to hang in the city centers during a time when racism was still prevalent. When you're excluded from mainstream events, you create your

Pieces by the Chrome Angelz in Covent Garden, 1985 (credits Pride TCA)

own gatherings. Gradually, the Black audience started to move into the city centre, and that's when it began to have an impact on the white community, particularly those open-minded white kids who were willing to cross over to the other side of the tracks, so to speak.

Yankee ▶ In London, we saw Hip Hop as a fusion of various cultures coming together and breaking down barriers.

Dolby D ▶ The main thing we were about was busking. And there were a lot of kids from the inner-city doing this dance, that was the thing, you could actually make some money doing this amazing dance from the hood.

Basil ▶ We were little kids making money, you know what I mean? We're not nicking from shops or anything like that, we're using our talent. But at the same time, we're linking with other people. So that's how we started, with different people from different areas, and with some people the links became strong.

Remedee ▶ Each area was very territorial, so going to Covent Garden and meeting up and communicating was also where we got information.

Fraggle ▶ Covent Garden was a place for tourists who loved our performances. It was new, it was exciting, but the police never saw it that way. They would arrest you and take you to Bold Street which was based around the corner.

Dolby D ▶ Covent has a history of street performers, street artists, from the time it was made and conceived. From impersonators, fire eaters, jugglers, magicians, Charlie Chaplin imitators and all sorts. But then in the 80s the

MC Remeedee
(CookieCrew)

street dancers arrived on the scene. This was the main spot. Look at the floor! It's not an easy floor, if you can do it here you can do it anywhere.

MC Mello ▶ I remember the first Saturday that I ever went to Covent Garden. I can remember being really excited for the whole journey. I was only about fourteen and there I was riding the train. So, I'm looking at all the stops and I'm full of excitement and anticipation as I see my stop getting closer and closer. I get out at Charing Cross, walk along The Strand and head up into Covent where you hit the cobblestones and then it opens up and straight away. I remember seeing some of the UK's best poppers, Dolby D was there, Micron, all the guys I'd seen in Freez's "I.O.U." video are right there in front of me. I'm enthusiastic.

MC Duke ▶ On certain Saturdays, even two or three hundred people could show up – body poppers, b-boys, writers, and others who simply wanted to be part of the scene.

Yankee ▶ Word of mouth was quite big at that time. In youth culture, things spread very quickly, and Covent Garden was the main drum, it was the Nyabinghi drum that was beating up all of London. You went there to find out about the parties, find out where to go. You come to Covent Garden and you would just speak to people and they would give you the information about what was happening.

Alex Mac ▶ when we started really hanging around in Covent there was no sort of real graffiti, street art or

MC Duke, 1985 (credits MC Duke).

anything out there. There was some boarding provided by the Opera House which basically had loads of posters on them and it sort of stretched just along the front of a kind of derelict piece of land and it wasn't until early '84 when the Opera House gave permission for people to paint on these boards that we started seeing some of the artists getting involved. So they were the first real, proper walls that a lot of people had seen in public. There was lots of graffiti going on locally, a lot of people who had their own halls of fame, down in Westbourne Grove and the Westway, up in East Ham, up in North, up in South, they all had various places where people were painting. So once the board started going up, they started pulling in more of the writers into Covent Garden.

MC Mello ▶ Covent Garden represented the heart, the core of Hip Hop culture in London. It's the centre, where we would come from all over London to congregate here, to have b-boying, the graffiti, the conversations, the debates. All of that stuff would take place here, and we would be all mirrors for each other, reflecting that b-boy, reflecting that Hip Hop, continuing that energy and that life. And if you were coming from other neighbourhoods, when you came here to Covent Garden you found people who had the same love for the same thing you did. So the love for Hip Hop was the thing that gelled everybody. It was unifying energy for all of us here, no matter the age, the gender, the class, the creed, the colour of skin, the ethnicity, it didn't matter, this was the place, this was the proving ground, this is where you come and show and prove what you can do, and you'd be respected and honoured based on your ability and your integrity.

Fraggle ▶ One day, I will never forget, we were by the cobbles in Covent Garden just hanging out and jamming and I will never forget that we just heard "uuuuu" and it just got louder and louder, and the next thing I understood is that there were the skinheads, and it was terrible. Hundreds and hundreds of skinheads came out of nowhere and they just started beating up everyone.

Yankee ▶ We had what we called warriors, there was a group of warriors who protected people in Covent Garden, because we used to get attacks from Skinheads, racist northerners who used to come to London to support their team. It was up to us to actually protect the environment. We met fists to fists.

DOLBY D VS ROCKSTEADY CREW

Basically this is the story of when Dolby D met the Rock Steady Crew! So I've come into the circle now, and boom, who do I see in front of me? The whole Rock Steady Crew, every last one of them, the whole "Hey You the Rock Steady Crew". You've got Crazy Legs, Ken Swift, Buck 4, Kuriaki, Doze and Baby Love, the whole crew. So, I was going up to them to actually show them love and respect, yeah, and to tell them "I watch you guys every day before I come out of my house, sincerely, yeah, and today was no different". But as I say this, they gave me the New York attitude, didn't they? "I heard you want to battle?" At the time if someone said "battle" this was when the crowd turns into an angry mob and all they want to see is a battle and someone burnt. I understand that, it's ok. So there's like battle, no one could hear anything, so I backed up to my corner. And this was here, as you see it's on a slight slope, as you see it's the cobblestones and what not. But this is where I live, they're just tourists here. So the battles kick off. Crazy Legs has come in first, doing a bit of toprock, his footwork, and he did his classic where he curls up in a ball freeze, the same thing he did in Wild Style. Do you know how many times I've watched Wild Style? Anyway, he's done that on me, so I came out, did some footwork, then a freeze or whatever, like "yeah, what?", Ken Swift came out now, he's giving me the Wild Style as well! Now don't get me wrong, Ken Swift, gangster gangster, the b-boy's b-boy, but he's giving me the Wild Style, the gangster freeze, he's done the swipes on me, and he's finished on me just like in Wild Style. I was like "oh ok Kenny, I've got something for you Kenny!" and I've done a couple of swipes, dicked him, went down again like that, dicked him again, dick all up in your face Kenny, what?! This is London Town! So then Buck Four comes up now, the Turtle master now, but this is Covent Garden, you see the cobblestones, he's all cautious on it, and he's treating lightly but I know every nook and cranny here, and I was like brrrrrr and that, I came out, dicked him as well, like what?! So now Kuriaki has come out, yeah? So I think "oh, this is going on, this is going on!". Now don't get me wrong, I don't think that I'm better than them, but you gotta pay to play, I know the way yeah? But now as back in the days, the police came along, and have broken everything up. And they've been ushered off to where they need to be, which was a little studio or something just over there, in Covent Garden, and so the battle went down, but it didn't really finish. So it wasn't like a fall-out battle, I'm sure I would have got burnt in the end, but I prepped my set.

MC Mello ▶ Under the Charing Cross tube train station there's a walkway vital to us because this is where we used to go to practice. We would practise here, the b-boys would practice breaking, the poppers and the boogaloo guys would be practising back here. There are some reflective glasses, this is what we'd use as our dance studio mirror so we could see what we're doing. If you remember the movie Beat Streets when they had that battle in the underground (New York City Breakers vs the Rock Steady), for us being teenagers under here we would have our little kind of vibe in battle you know what I'm saying. This is another iconic part that is connected to the Covent Garden scene, and the whole b-boy and Hip Hop scene in London.

At that point, Hip Hop was starting to define its own symbolic places, transforming the social geography of the city. Every weekend, young people poured into the streets of the West End, following what seemed like a mandatory route: Covent Garden as the first stop, then lunch at *Quick Burger* in Leicester Square, followed by the classic tour in Soho at

Groove Records, the record store with imported music only, to finally arrive at Spats on 37 Oxford Street, an afternoon disco open from 12 to 3 PM, known as the first Hip Hop hub of the scene.

MC Mello ▶ Spat was a very important club for Hip Hop, in Oxford street on Saturdays afternoon. Westwood was the main DJ for Spat. Westwood is old school and he was very instrumental for the evolution of Hip Hop. you'd see the biggest battle and MCs partying up the place, poppers doing their thing, writers etc. You could also network inside there. And as soon as it was over everyone was going to Covent Garden and hang out the rest of the night.

Linton Lee ▶ And on Saturdays, there was a club called Spats. Little small, tiny club, which I'm sure used to break the fire code laws. They'd just cram everybody in there. And it was where everybody started doing all their battles, and dancing, and just chilling out, it was an afternoon club for Hip Hoppers basically.

Rodney P ▶ Spats was the place where any Hip Hop kid wanted to hang out and be there.

Tim Westwood was the resident DJ at Spats, while the four Family Quest MCs were the *Masters of Ceremony* of those legendary afternoons: Cheeko, MC E = mix, Dirty Harry and Mystery MC (the first female MC in the UK). The group had sent Tim Westwood a demo with a single track on it, to be played on his radio show on LWR. Westwood was impressed and invited them to perform live on the club

stage. That performance thrilled the audience and convinced Westwood to collaborate with them. Family Quest is also credited with recording the first Rap song with a British accent, *Outer Space 84 Rap*, released in 1984 on the *Jungle Rhythm* label.

E=mix ▶ Tim Westwood asked us to come and we went there with that one rap and Tim Westwood played *Sucker MCs* and we rhymed over it. We all felt great about what we had done; all of a sudden he played another song and he said "yeah carry on, carry on!" so we all looked at each other "what are we going to do?" But being thrown in the deep end like that was one thing that was crucial,

Family Quest MCs: Cheeko, Mystery MC, Dirty Harry & MC E=mix
(credits Henry Chalfant)

because now we just had to come off with something,
and everything we did from that point was off the top
of our head and we went on for the whole session, we
walked out from there thinking "we can really do this"
So Family Quest was actually born and sorted. Then Tim
Westwood had to pull out and we took over Spats for the
next couple of years. It grew into the home of UK Hip
Hop because people would travel from as far as Scotland
to come down to this place.

In the second half of the 1980s, sound systems, cassettes,
videotapes, pirate radios and clubs, operating on multiple
levels, allowed the London scene to exponentially expand its
own sphere of influence. This burgeoning scene was further
bolstered by the success of two key events in 1985: *Electro
Rock*, a showcase of Hip Hop artists held at the Hippodrome
in Leicester Square in March, and *Freestyle '85*, a self-managed
festival organized by young enthusiasts in Covent Garden on

December 14th. These events highlighted how the embryonic scene, now laying solid foundations, was consolidating a larger community.

Early Shows

Electro Rock, recorded during an event at the Hippodrome, a nightclub in Leicester Square, in March 1985, represented a sort of showcase of the Hip Hop artists who had energised the scene in recent months. Presented by Mike Allen, a DJ of *Capital Radio*, the video features performances of Breaking, Popping, Beatboxing as well as the performances of MCs, DJs and b-boys, including Family Quest, Dizzi Heights, Mastermind Roadshow and the London Allstars. The international guest of the evening was Afrika Bambaataa.

> **Dizzi Heights** ▶ In America you had a film like *Wild Style* which is a cult-pop film. In Britain we've done a thing called "Hip Hop at the Hippodrome" [Electro Rock] which was a film made on a really low budget and I was proud to be part of. It's basically a good example of British work. There are a couple of British rappers on it, then we've got Afrika Bambaataa's on it, and of course Americans are always on top of the bill, but the best part of it is the amount of break dancers from all over England. Not many things were captured from that era because back then it was a word of mouth and experience.

Electro Rock alternates on-stage performances with backstage footage. On stage, the artists performed all their originality and skills, while rapping with the microphone in hand,

Dizzi Heights on stage at the Hippodrome during Electro Rock, London 1985 (credits Martin Jones)

mixing and scratching records on the turntables, or dancing on stage, highlighting a style that had nothing to envy from its American counterpart. In the backstage footage, on the other hand, we see them joking with each other, practising improvised freestyle sessions, and even celebrating Mystery MC's birthday, the only woman performing on stage. These shots are an important document as they bring out all the swagger, the innocence and the passion that drove them. The scene was still small, and those artists were truly friends who had contributed to its creation from the very beginning. But we should not underestimate the element of competition, especially among the b-boys from across the nation. One battle, in particular, is hard to forget, where the Popper Basil Pepperpot annihilates his opponent with a series of dance moves.

Dolby D ▶ In Electro Rock, you see the first happening of all of the UK coming together. London All Stars, the b-boys from Wolverhampton, Broken Glass from Manchester, Nottingham Rock City Crew, that was a very big happening. Somebody wanted to document what was going on and they basically found a venue, the Hippodrome, put it all together, filmed it. We didn't know that would be only testimony of Britain's legacy to Hip Hop, you know what I mean, to British Hip Hop and breakdancing.

Jonzi D ▶ I remember Electro Rock because I couldn't get in. I was outside. I remember being outside there and there was more of a buzz outside. Hip Hop culture was there, we was in one of the biggest most famous venues in London at the time, the Hippodrome. And I remember being outside, there was police out there because they've never seen so many young Black kids in one area at the same time ever before.

James McNally ▶ In 1985 you had all these people that have been devoting to Hip Hop for the preceding four years or so and they're kind of gaining this momentum and this is really the kind of big extravaganza for all of them. Then after this, you've got the Cookie Crew who won the crew section of Tim Westwood's rap competition at the Wag Club. They're part of a slightly newer generation coming through, like MC Mell'O, who about a year later would be turning from popping to rapping.

Alex Mac ▶ Freestyle '85 was born out of the centre (a community centre in Charing Cross) where a young

London All Stars performing at the Hippodrome during Electro Rock, London 1985 (credits Martin Jones)

Canadian, Steven Laforge also known as the Buddha of the Canadian Floormasters, was working as a social worker. As part of a youth program, he pulled together some of the youth to set up an event, get sponsors, think about the business of running it, and actually get it together. It culminated in an event at the Jubilee Hall, in Covent Garden, an afternoon of shows, Bboys and rapping.

Sparkii Ski ▶ We all used to hang out in one of the homeless shelters/youth clubs attached to the West End. If it was rainy or cold or we were bored, there was this place called the Centre. They've got a few of them around the city and they've got one next to St Martin on the Fields. We all used to hang out there. There was a generation of Covent Garden people and Leicester Square people who used to hook up there. They had a hall, a dance studio,

A winter afternoon in 1985 inside The Centre, St. Martins on the Fields (credits Stephen Buddha Leafloor)

a gym, I used to play in a band and we would go there because there was also a little rehearsal room.

Buddha ▶ We put together a committee for Freestyle 85 and it turned possibly into one of the most important Hip Hop events of the early UK scene. The organising committee had to interact, listening to each other's opinions because we had representatives from the MCs, from the Graf community, the DJs and the b-boys and they had to talk and respect each other. We didn't want to do it in Brixton, we could do it in Covent Garden, in the heart of the city where a lot of people would hang. We wanted the people involved in Hip Hop to tell their story in their own terms.

Pride ▶ At the time, we just really wanted to put a jam together, it wasn't anything more than that. We weren't thinking, this is going to be big. And I guess part of it was not really understanding the impact of what we were doing and that we were having outside our own community. All of the sudden, we saw hundreds of people queuing up. And for me, I was like "is this something that we've created?" I was just glad to be part of it, and I was working alongside my peers.

Alex Mac ▶ It was quite a seminal event in that nothing of this nature had been seen in London. So Freestyle happened in December '85 and I think there was a natural progression onto bigger events.

E=mix ▶ Because the scene was very new, there were a number of events taking place and people wanted acts to fill the events.

The other notable event of the period to mention is UK Fresh '86, a legendary Hip Hop concert held at Wembley Arena in the summer of 1986. Organised by Mike Allen of Capital Radio and DJ Dave Pearce of BBC Radio, in collaboration with Street Sounds, Morgan Khan's record label, is still remembered today as the biggest Rap concert held on British soil.

The list of artists was a *who's who* of the American scene with Grandmaster Flash & The Furious Five, DJ Cheese and Word of Mouth, Captain Rock, Aleem, Lovebug Starski, Afrika Bambaataa, Mantronix, Steady B, The Real Roxanne, Sir Mix-a-Lot. The only British artists were Mastermind Roadshow, Family Quest and Hardrock Soul Movement.

James McNally ▶ Fresh '86 was put together by Capital Radio as part of the Capital Radio Festival with Morgan

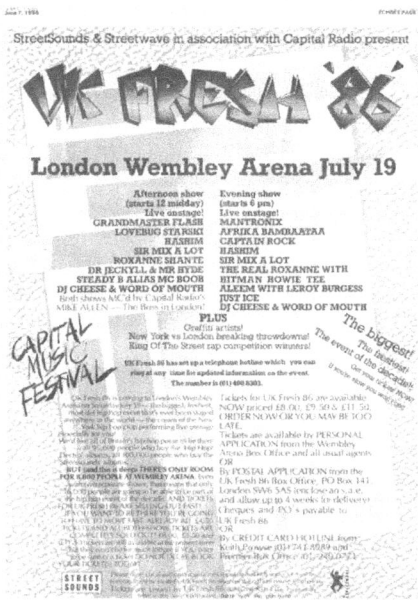

Advertisement for UK Fresh '86 published on the pages of "Echoes" magazine on June 7, 1986

Khan's Street Sounds label. They put together a lot of big US artists onto a London stage at Wembley Arena and showcased them. These were some of the artists appearing on Morgan Kahn's electro albums.

Linton Lee ▶ UK Fresh '86 at the Wembley Arena was the first time we got to see all of these people we were listening to, on one stage. And it was just mind-blowing.

Rodney P ▶ There were events that really changed my life and UK Fresh was one of them. They had all the leading artists in Hip Hop music at the time; it was sponsored by Street Sounds. At the time the Street Sounds albums were life changing. We would wait for them, they were compilation albums that would have the 20 most popular

Hip Hop tunes of the time, and a lot of them would be Electro tunes. None of us had a ticket to get in but we thought that being the real UK Hip Hop scene, we had a right to be there so we went there and attacked the building to find a way to get in. If there were an event that said it represented Hip Hop, it couldn't exist without us.

E=mix ▶ UK Fresh is still the biggest Hip Hop event ever to be staged in this country, and there's been nothing like it since.

Cheeko ▶ After that event, it was very much a move into Rap, and DJing and the other elements started to disappear so much.

Skam One ▶ I think from the mid '80s everything kind of went its own separate way. Hip Hop was kind of broken up into like, you know, graffiti started doing, you know, they went off in one direction, rappers and DJs went off in another direction, Hip Hop stopped mixing as a whole movement.

In the mid-1980s, London's Hip Hop scene was primarily expressed through the Breaking and Popping performances at Covent Garden, the battles between MCs at Spats, jams at the Africa Centre and the weekly succession of warehouse parties. Always accompanied by the loudest mixers and speakers, live gatherings were the determining factor. While radio and the first vinyls also played a role, if the culture of sound systems hadn't already paved the streets for so many years, British Hip Hop would have been something else entirely.

THE NOREIK

834 SEVEN SISTERS ROAD, N.15

Open 5 Nights Weekly Wednesday to Sunday

COMMENCING

SUNDAY 15th MAY 1977

LATE SESSION DOWNSTAIRS

for 18's and over, only

MUSIC BY

JAH SUFFERER   FAT MAN HI-FI
JAH SHAKA   v

SUNDAY 22nd MAY 1977

JAH SUFFERER

v

● MOA ANBASSA ●

SUNDAY 29th MAY 1977

JAH SUFFERER

v

FEDERAL HI-FI

EVERY SUNDAY - VARIOUS COMPETITIONS - GATE RAFFLES
ALSO VARIOUS LIVE SHOWS

Every Sun. & Thurs. Ladies Adm. Free with Membership Cards

LICENSED BAR AND RESTAURANT

TUBE & TRAINS to SEVEN SISTERS   Buses 149, 259, 243, 279, 97, 41, 230, 76, 73

Sound System Culture

A Bit of History

In the 1930s, in the African American communities, music played from the speakers of the phonograph or the jukebox was among the most popular forms of entertainment in road-house clubs, juke joints, as well as outdoor settings or private parties. Especially in Jamaican music culture, the various possibilities arose from the reproduction of recorded music that had further evolved through sound systems.

A sound system is "a mobile and amplified audio repro-duction system, managed by a team with the aim of creating a party atmosphere wherever you are", including on the streets and in public places.

Born in Jamaica in the 1940s within working-class com-munities as a form of social gathering during parties and other special occasions, by the mid-1950s, sound systems had evolved into a sophisticated form of mobile entertainment, rivalling and sometimes replacing professional musicians' live performances. Sound systems were in fact large and powerful setups, specifically built to play records as an alternative to expensive live orchestras.

These collectives, known as sound systems, were promoted by groups that encompassed all the necessary skills for their management: the operator who managed the controls; the selecter who decided which records to play; the DJ who could speak while playing records, the engineer who took care of the sound system, and the security and transportation staff, which often consisted in a group of kids willing to contribute in any way possible to be part of the team, and known as the *box boys*. Organising parties and selling food and drinks provided an alternative source of income and it also served as a way to keep money within the community.

Furthermore, the entrepreneurial spirit that character-ised those individuals gave to sound systems a meaning that went beyond mere musical entertainment. Sound system operators were able to understand the tastes and desires of the audience in front of them, people who had worked hard throughout the week, just to earn a few pennies and being able to party on the weekends.[1] A skilled soundman knew that the audience had high expectations, and if he failed to satisfy them, many wouldn't hesitate to make it known. The audience was usually just a little over a metre away from the sound system, leaving a little room for the soundman to hide.

Simon Jones ▶ The sound system first and foremost is a technical system for reproducing recorded music. We're

---

[1] Lloyd Bradley in www.bl.uk/windrush/articles/sound-systems

talking about a communal public entertainment institution. When we're talking about the Reggae sound systems which originated in Jamaica, the nearest equivalent would be a mobile discotheque. We're talking about a much more sophisticated institution or cultural formation which made up a whole multiplicity of performance practices. It has its own aesthetics, it has its own craft technologies for making the actual equipment and delivering recorded sound. A sound system is a network of social networks, teams of people who have a specific division of labour. It's also the focus of cultural economies for actually making money. But at the heart of the sound system are a set of performance practices, live performance practices, which create a multilayered soundscape made up of recorded songs, processed and re-performed in a live context. Among the various sound processing techniques, such as mixing and sound effects, an additional layer is introduced through live DJing or Toasting, which includes live singing, various spoken interjections, and announcements. When all these elements come together, they create a complex, multi-layered polyvocal soundscape. The sound system developed in the Jamaican context and it developed into a kind of musical laboratory, a testbed of musical innovation out of which all the major musical movements in Jamaican popular music came. You have this unique relationship, this dynamic relationship between the audience, musicians, sound engineer and performers working in that kind of close interrelationship.

The combination of DIY skills, innovation, entrepreneurial spirit and a sense of identity transformed sound systems into the beating heart of the music scene, with operators constantly seeking for new exclusive songs and remixes to play in order to outshine the competition. Later on, they started producing records exclusively for their own project.

Since the 1950s, the culture of sound systems in Great Britain found an audience eager for music, parties and gathering spaces, leading to the birth of an underground circuit of Blues and home parties, and impromptu Dance Halls. Thanks to their ability to combine instrumental versions of songs or exclusive dubplates – unreleased singles played for the first time live – with the lyrical performance of toasters, the sound system culture represents an important role in both Jamaican and British history.[2]

Upon their arrival in the United Kingdom during the first wave, immigrants from the West Indies brought their traditions, and it didn't take long before the first *shebeens* or Blues parties were organised in private residences or basements as a regular Saturday night party for Caribbean workers who were excluded from traditional entertainment venues. Racism came as a surprise to the Caribbean population, who had been taught to consider Britain as the glorious motherland. However, since their arrival, they were directed towards low-paying jobs with precarious working conditions and subjected to discriminatory extortion: for example, they were placed in dilapidated accommodations and relegated to a subpar education system. To their great surprise, a *colour barrier* was erected between Black people and the rest of British society. "There was this strong sense of empire, we were all British. For my parents' generation, to find out they weren't considered truly British, it was a real shock. They were just Blacks".[3]

[2] Lloyd Bradley, Sounds Like London, cit.
[3] Interview with Diane Abbott in Mike e Trevor Phillips, *Windrush: The*

MC Duke ▶ The British government first asked people to come over from the Caribbean, because there weren't enough men here after the war, so they needed people to run the trains, sweep the streets, run the buses; they asked loads of people from the Caribbean to come to England. Everybody in the Caribbean are hard workers so they were like "Yeah let's go there, let's work. They've offered us a chance to better our lives' so they took the opportunity". That wasn't confined to just Jamaica, it was all across the Caribbean, they actually got resources, i.e. people, to come all over the Caribbean.

The import of Jamaican music was initially managed by the immigrants themselves. The spaces where it could be listened to were apartments, illegal venues, and a few night clubs. By paying the entrance fee, one could listen to the latest hit records, enjoy good food, and have a few drinks.

> You had a lot of shebeens, you call it that, a social situation of which there was nothing because of the no-coloured policy, no Blacks, no coloureds in homes, entertainments, there was nothing really for Black people so you had to create your own social environment. And a chap called Fullerton was a tailor and he bought his first house in Talbot Road. He had a basement and we used to have blues dances and stuff. Everybody used to get down there and get down. You had people like Duke Vin who used to play with big speakers.[4]

MC Duke ▶ Now, in Jamaica in slang that's called a "shebeens", it actually means "shove 'em in" as many

Irresistible Rise of Multi-Racial Britain, HarpersCollins, London 1998, p. 212.
    [4] Mike Phillips, Charlie Phillips, *Notting Hill in the Sixties*, Lawrence and Wishart, London 1991, pp. 52-55.

Jonzi D,
London
2013

people as you can so you'd get the money to pay the rent, do you understand me? Now, people obviously would mingle with people from other cultures, and they would say 'Come to this party!'. They would go to the party and they hear the music that people were playing from the Caribbean and so they started to influence the music that was getting played by other people here.

[...] we established our own independent cultural institutions, we established the blues dance, which would be held in somebody's house on a Saturday night. We established the culture of the Sound System and gave Reggae music a local agitation and a name in this country. My parents' generation had by then established little social clubs where people would meet for recreation, dances, play dominos, and this kind of things.[5]

DJ Fingers ▶ The reason why we had things like the blues dances and our own entertainment, was because

[5] Interview with Linton Kwesi Johnson, in Mike e Trevor Phillips, *Windrush*, cit., p. 298.

there was not such a concept like a club or something that we could easily frequent, so we organised our own sort of entertainment. I believe that throughout England you could go to any street, especially if there was the Afro-Caribbean community, and you would find a party.

Jonzi D ▶ So, the blues was an all-night Reggae session. There was one place we called The Dellow Street Blues, and the parties held there used to go on until daylight, the next morning. They would be selling alcohol I guess illegally, and you would smell the best herb in the area. The blues, it's directly coming from the West Indian experience.

James McNally ▶ Basically what happens in a blues dance is like emptying out a room, taking all the chairs and sofas out, having maybe a single red light bulb in the corner, a little kind of turntable set up with some speakers, and then you'd have like a little bar somewhere and you'd buy some drinks from the cash and carry and sell. So, you'd have a little nightclub in someone's house or in an abandoned building somewhere.

Without the music, without the Friday night shebeens and the Saturday night parties, I don't know what we would have done as a people. It held us together. It really did. It held us together in those days, I mean, we were moving from Ska to Rocksteady, you know and the Rocksteady was so warm and sweet it took us right back to the Caribbean. You needed something to take you from the pressures of the climate, situation, the culture, the food, the hostility against you as a man of colour. And the music for a brief moment of a Saturday night takes us back to the Caribbean. We could talk, we could intermingle, we could dance, and we could just feel the groove. Very, very important, the only thing that pulls us together is our colour and the music; and the only thing that takes us away from the day to day jobs of life is the music on a Saturday night.[6]

Ishmahil Blagrove ▶ When people first arrived here in the UK because of racism and discrimination, people from the Caribbean or West Indies couldn't go to pubs, bars, events and socialise in safe spaces. So they gathered in people's homes during the weekends or after work. It was a very busy house scene because there were no other spaces where they could socialise. In those spaces, people played cards, dominos, gambles, and when you're there you eat; they were people cooking food. In those spaces, some would turn on the blue spot gram and play some music or would have some records imported from Jamaica. These were the places where people started mingling instead of sticking to people from the same island. That became a social scene, those house parties were known as Blues Dance.

After a week of hard work, a house party complete with curried rice and goat curry, beer or rum, brought together immigrants of various nationalities, helping them realize they shared more in common than what might have set them apart.

Simon Jones ▶ Sound Systems started appearing in the mid '50s, around 1955. Two sound systems were very

[6] Interview with Mike Nesbeth in Mike e Trevor Phillips, *Windrush*, cit., pp. 299-300.

formative in the British context, Duke Vin and Count Suckle. The sound system tradition was brought to the UK by Jamaican working class migrants and recreated in a British urban context and adapted to it in the form of the Blues parties, the shebeens that took place in basements, in private dwellings and in various settings like town halls and nightclubs. It evolved as an alternative legit space, as a response to racism and to that kind of segregation in the legit sphere. Sound systems evolved as an alternative media channel, an alternative broadcasting channel for music imported from the Caribbean.

Although the first wave of immigrants included communities from multiple Caribbean nations, Jamaicans accounted for about 60 percent of them, and the majority coming primarily from the rural areas of the island. In the second wave of the mid-1950s, Jamaicans still constituted the majority, but this time the immigrants mostly came from urban contexts and belonged to the working class. It was this latter group that brought with them those early Jamaican cultural practices, with the most significant being the sound system.

The pioneers of this scene were two friends, Vincent George Forbes (Duke Vin) and Wilbert Augustus Campbell (Earl Suckle), who arrived in London in 1952, after travelling as stowaways on a ship carrying bananas. Duke Vin found accommodation in West London, in the Ladbroke Grove area, and founded the first sound system called *Duke Vin and the Ticklers*, in 1955. Shortly after, a few months later, Count Suckle followed suit. Both adopted the Kingston model, following the example of *Tom the Great Sebastian*, whom they had worked for, thus starting a war of watts and decibels. When Duke Vin powered up his sound system for the first time in the streets of London, with an unprecedented wall of speakers, a second-hand turntable, and a microphone, it became the rallying call for a community in search for a new identity.

Ishmahil Blagrove ▶ Duke Vin started the first sound system in Britain around 1955. Around that time there was a Grenadian guy called Mr. Eddie. He was an engineer, and he could build amplifiers; Duke asked him to build amplifiers for him and the rest is history. Those early arrivals from the Caribbean to Britain, they were playing jazz, soul, RnB American popular music. They were heavily influenced by American music but these DJs would play an eclectic mix.

Although much of the musical equipment used in Jamaica was directly shipped from the UK – such as *Warfdale* and *Eagle* loudspeakers, GEC Holborn's *KT88* and *KT66* valves – British companies never took the technical specifications of Jamaican soundmen seriously, unintentionally fueling the rise of local artisans, especially carpenters and electricians. The audio systems of those early sound systems were made entirely handcrafted using wood sourced from old cabinets, furniture or construction scraps. Thus, fathers and uncles mentored their children and nephews, passing down the art of self-building sound systems.

BUILDING STACKS

Much has been written about the origins, history and key figures of the sound system scene, but rarely do we find in-depth discussions about those artisans, true sound scientists, who built speakers and custom amplifiers capable of delivering tremendous power to those systems. While it is true that the basic elements of a sound system remain the same – a turntable, with purists favouring the Garrard 4HF, a stack of amps, and an array of speakers – it is the customizations of these devices that truly set one sound system apart from another, in addition to the music selection.

One of the legendary builders of the London scene was Shortman, the son of a Jamaican carpenter. His passion for music technology had driven him since his teenage years to eagerly wait for his father to finish work so he could seize his tools and try to build speakers. His first attempt was quite comical. Shortman himself recalls the episode: "For a friend's birthday in Brixton, I built a large speaker without using screws or glue, only nails. Halfway through the party, it fell apart!".[7] However, the experience didn't discourage him; on the contrary, the young engineer quickly learned from those mistakes. In the following months, he gained the experience and reputation by working on the setups of various local sound systems, from Sir Higgins to Frontline International. Over the years, his list of clients expanded. His speakers had become bigger, more and more powerful, especially with the emergence of sound systems like Iration Steppas, Jah Tubbys or Aba Shanti-I in the 1990s. For Shortman, if the music carried a message, then that message had to resonate everywhere like a jackhammer. However, the true spiritual father of all London sound engineers was Metroman, a character as legendary as he was mysterious, considered a true master in the creation of valve amplifiers and custom speakers. Metroman, not yet a teenager, discovered that his cousin Tom was the famous *Tom The Great Sebastian*, one of the founding fathers of the Jamaican sound system scene. His visceral love for music led him to leave school at the young age of 14 and work as an installer of Mercury radios, which were considered more like precious ornaments than

---

[7] http://www.dub-stuy.com/sound-sculptors-london-sound-system-builders.

everyday objects. What fascinated him were the *glass bottles* found inside the radios. Those bottles were valves, referring to the period before transistors.

He tried to satisfy his curiosity by disassembling and reassembling them several times, using a self-made circuit diagram published in an American electronic magazine as his guide. Just as he was starting to make a name for himself in Jamaica, he had moved with his family to England. It was in 1957, and while sound systems were rapidly becoming the musical *phenomenon* of the time, Metroman immediately realised that the scene in England was almost non-existent. It was a bitter discovery, but it seemed to motivate him even more. His mission would be to build an amplifier worthy of those used by the sound systems of Coxsone and Duke Reid. He immediately set to work by discovering *Voltection*, a company that manufactured radio amplifiers located a short bus ride away from London. That amplifier wasn't bad, a good starting point, although it certainly wasn't what he was looking for. After a few months, he began testing it in the basement of a bar run by notorious gangsters from the East London area, the *Kray Twins*, experimenting with the speakers he built using reclaimed wood found at construction sites where he worked during the day.

He had bought inexpensive resistors, capacitors and lamps on Tottenham Court Road and dismantled the amplifier piece by piece and then soldered it back together, by adding components and power, improvising when he didn't know what to do. A year later, his amps sounded better and were more powerful than those his compatriots imported straight from Jamaica.

He would become one of the very first sound systems in England, initially playing in the Kray's venue and then travelling from location to location, from city to city under the name of *Tune Waver*. It later became *Metro the Tune Waver Downbeat*, known simply as Metro by most. Crowds flocked to the venues where he played until 1967 when, due to a piece of glass hitting his eye during a fight at a party where he was performing, he became partially blind and was forced to retire from the scene.

In 1969, Metro met a young soundman at a club in North London; the young man's name was Jah Shaka, a future icon of the English Roots Reggae scene. Metroman built for him the first amplifier *not for personal use*. That custom piece, with its unmatched, unique and powerful sound, is one of the reasons for Jah Shaka's success.

In London, when it comes to the art of building stacks, the name of Metroman still resonates today.

Cheeko ▶ What would make one sound system different from another, what made them peculiar, was how the speaker boxes looked; everyone designed their speakers to suit their taste. Secondly it would be the sound effects, so most sounds built their own sound effects. And another thing would be the way MCs would toast on the microphone, how they would announce their sound. So that was a big thing as well and that made everyone identify with one sound or another. It was sound effects, the way your speaker boxes looked and even sometimes the way members of each sound system would dress, so there was a code.

Although there were a few night clubs run by Jamaicans in Soho, the central areas of the city remained out of reach for more recently arrived immigrants. Some London pubs welcomed Caribbean customers and even allowed sound systems to play on weekends, but beyond a few exceptions, there was an open hostility and much of the nightlife was off-limits to Black men. The Black community used music to bridge that gap in their imagination between the lives they left behind and the circumstances they faced. It was through these embryonic practices that Jamaican musical tradition spread throughout the Black communities in Great Britain.[8]

The Sound systems represented a safe space, both physically and spiritually, offering protection against the challenges posed by a hostile white society. These sound systems represented a sphere of autonomy, a hospitable enclave where individuals could redefine their dignity, reconstruct collective consciousness, and foster solidarity. Additionally, they evolved into arenas of resistance, serving as the sole outlets for the expression of their culture and political ideals.

DJ Devastate ▶ Sound systems were really the places where you got your street grades, if you weren't a Casanova or a Badman, then you had to be in a sound system!

By the end of the 1960s, there were sound systems in all major English cities; with many of them adopting names directly inspired by those already existing in Jamaica, just like Duke Reid and Coxsone. In London, the sound systems emerged primarily in Brixton, Lewisham, Notting Hill, Daltson, Hackney, Ladbroke Grove, Shepherd's Bush.

MC Mello ▶ The sound system culture was a permanent presence in the streets and served as a strong cultural force that brought people together. Each area had its own sound systems, which represented the neighborhood where they originated. When sound systems played against each other, it was neighborhood versus neighborhood, block against block.

[8] Simon Jones, *Black Culture, White Youth*, McMillan, New York 1988, p. 41.

The proliferation of sound systems facilitated the establishment of a sort of network, both at the city and national levels, characterised by competition. Each area had its own sound system, ready to challenge any other rival. In these battles, they competed against each other based on volume, sound quality and exclusive recordings known as *dubplates*, which aimed to conquer the crowd, the true and sole judge of these clashes. Sound systems travelled from neighbourhood to neighbourhood, from city to city, acting as mobile discos of the Afro-diasporic culture.

From the intimate blues parties of the 1950s to the thunderous sound systems of the 1960s, exemplified by Count Shelley, through the politically charged Reggae Roots movement of the 1970s, led by icons like Jah Shaka and Fatman, and culminating in the titans of the 1980s, such as Saxon and Frontline, sound systems have been the heartbeat of the ever-evolving grassroots musical cultures, with their journey commencing in the world of Reggae music. Since the moment the young Caribbean immigrant Duke Vincent Forbes created the first rudimentary sound system and began playing loud selections of Ska and Calypso songs, the sound systems have always been a reference point in the development of subsequent music cultures from bottom up, starting of course from Reggae.

The 1980 film *Babylon*, directed by Franco Rosso, is the first cinematic testimony of the Reggae sound system scene. Set in the gritty landscape of South East London, amidst the backdrop of impoverished and dangerous neighborhoods, like Deptford, characterised by massive housing estates and simmering racial tensions, the narrative follows the trials of a sound system called *Ital Lion*, as it prepares for a clash against one of the most popular sound of the area: *Jah Shaka*

(who plays himself). The search for exclusive dubplates fuels a subplot that brings to the forefront an underground economy and other distinctive elements of a scene that have never been documented before.

The immersion into the highly competitive reality of sound systems is experienced through the perspective of the protagonist, *Blue* – played by Brinsley Forde, lead singer of Aswad – charismatic DJ/toaster of *Ital Lion*. Blue's everyday life, just like that of many other young Black individuals, is filled with numerous challenges, including police harassment, a racist employer, and neighbours who seem to suffocate him with absurd demands and restrictions. As a result, the success of his sound system becomes his only escape and redemption. The director does not appear to have left anything to chance, as the description of the Black London at the time is as meticulous as it is bitter, reflecting the systemic nature of British racism. There are no filters in either celebration or condemnation. Due to a lack of having a budget to pay for extras, the filming includes real people engaged in their everyday activities, the pub patrons are real customers, just as the young people in line in front of the job centres are. The audience is immersed in raw footage amid informal conversations on various street topics and random situations. This makes it a highly significant historical document and a perfect representation of the 1980s scene.

Jonzi D ▶ The roots of the West Indian experience in England can be traced back to the sound systems and house parties. In these settings, the West Indian community can truly express itself. I believe that the sound system is the cornerstone of the entire beat-related music culture that has emerged in this country. It's in the West Indian blues, the underground parties, and the house gatherings that the West Indian community comes together in the face of racism.

Jazzie B ▶ The importance of the sound systems was far more than just playing music, it was your connection with people in the Caribbean. It was a refuge from everything that went on during your week at work, where you could be around like-minded people or where you could meet people, and it was how you expressed yourself. For the operator too, it was a business opportunity, and there were others that made money from around the sound systems, so it was a fusion of music, business and life, and something we were in control of for ourselves.[9]

Simon Jones ▶ The sound systems played a critical role in Britain, they provided the music and accompaniment to a whole array of social events within Britain's Black communities, life events, birthday parties, christenings, weddings, receptions, bank holiday outings, you name it. The sound system was there, providing the soundtrack. It was a cultural focal point. In many ways it acted as a social glue that kept communities together. It became as important as institutions like the church. All the places in which the sound systems played became, spaces of solidarity, spaces of celebration, of joy. A defensive enclave on the threat because all these spaces, beginning from the 1950s all the way through the current period, were suppressed by the authorities, by the police. They had to be defended. In political terms, we're referring to an alternative public sphere that evolved, nurturing political consciousness, especially during the 1970s when discussing the rise of youth sounds among second-generation Black Britons.

MC Mello ▶ For many of us, the Reggae sound system, tracing the sound, listening to the DJs, hearing the MCs and the chatters, was the foundation that honed our skills and truly shaped who we became, be it in our lyrical or musical expressions, our attitude, or our cultural identity.

[9] JazzieB in Lloyd Bradley, *Sounds Like London*, Serpent's Tail, London, 2013, pp 8-9.

London thus became the scene for a transformation fuelled by diasporic culture, triggering a process of urban renewal and redefinition of social identities that would shake the paradigms of English culture. This shift towards the periphery, led by those who had previously been marginalized, brought marginality to the forefront of popular culture and youth entertainment.

Lovers Rock

By the mid-1970s, some British sound systems began to drift away from the strictly roots Reggae scene; this was possible thanks to the birth of *Lovers Rock*, a new musical genre more in tune with the tastes and aspirations of young Black Londoners. It's interesting to note how *Lovers Rock* is actually the first form of indigenous Reggae, born when sound systems started recording and playing romantic ballads sung by young Black women. In 1974, producer Count Shelly released the first song, Ginger Williams' *Tenderness*, and the following year saw Louisa Mark's hit *Caught You in a Lie*, a Reggae interpretation of an obscure Soul song produced by Dennis Bovell for the Lloyd Coxsone sound system. Records were self-released, featuring Reggae covers of Motown and Philadelphia soul ballads, creating a perfect mix of Reggae, Soul, R'n'B, with a touch of Disco music. While Jamaican music has always been influenced by American Soul, *Lovers Rock* went far beyond the boundaries that defined the two genres, blending the soft sounds of Soul music with the powerful bass lines and the uplifting rhythm of Reggae.

Lovers Rock seemed to embody the aspirations for integration and social mobility of those young people who wanted

PEBBLES PRESENTS
A

M U S I C A L ★
★SPECTACULAR

ON
Saturday 4th August 1979

AT THE
NEWLANDS CLUB
HIGH WYCOMBE, BUCKS

★ ★ ★ ★ ★★ ★ ★ ★ ★

Bubbling to the Universal
★ *Field Marshall* ★
★ ★ **SIR COXSONE** ★ ★

★★★★★★   ★★★★★★

also 1979 Black Echoes Award Winner
★ ★ **FATMAN HI-FI** ★ ★

Door open 7.30pm   Dont miss this night of sheer entertainment
Trains leaves Frequently from Paddington Station

Flyer for Sir Coxsone's party, 1979

to dress elegantly, be successful at work and choose the soundtrack of their days. The contrast between the sounds from Jamaica and the sumptuous love songs of *Lovers Rock* are the most appropriate metaphor to understand what was happening in those times in London.

Simon Jones ▶ The origins of Lovers' Rock in Britain can be pinpointed fairly precisely to the mid1970s. We're talking about the 4 Aces in Dalston, Coxsone Sound. Coxsone used to play lots of Soul and Reggae; had a large following among young Black women. Talent contests used to be held at the 4 Aces where members of the audience, particularly young women, would perform Reggae versions of soul and RnB classic. As I understand it, the person creating the rhythm tracks for the talent contexts was Andy Ravel, who is one of the prime movers in the origins of Lovers' Rock in Britain. That's where it started and Lovers' Rock as a genre reconciled, fusing the popularity of Soul and Reggae and very much a movement of Black young women asserting their taste, their identity, their experiences through the music as performers and as a listening and dancing audience. It's correct to say that it was also a response to the more masculine aspects of roots Reggae, the style of dancing, the themes of roots Reggae which didn't always necessarily speak to the experiences of women.

Don Letts ▶ I think the other major thing that really fuelled its creation was the fact that around about the early to mid '70s, the Reggae coming out in Jamaica was very militant, very politicised which was very much a reflection of the social and economic climate, political climate. Those political, militant messages seemed to transfer perfectly to the streets of London. The mid '70s, it was tough, man. We had the riots, the right-wing party, The National Front. Yeah, if you were Black in those days, it was pretty rough. Anyway, you've got all this militant, politicised music coming up, coming out of Jamaica. But the truth of the matter is, for my generation – first-generation British-born Black – we were pretty young. We were in our mid-teens, early 20s. More interested in matters of the heart. We're starting to fall in love, starting to have relationships. Truth be told, we weren't fighting all the time. You wanted to make love or whatever. It's also about that expression of a more emotional side of the Black experience in the UK.[10]

[10] Don Letts interview: https://reggae-steady-ska.com/sweet-romance-don-letts-talks-lovers-rock.

Lovers Rock quickly spread to cities like Birmingham, Leeds and Bristol, wherever there were Black communities. While many songs spoke about the experience of young Blacks on the streets of the cities, the most widespread theme was certainly love in all its forms.

Don Letts ▶ Lovers Rock was integral to the journey of Black British people in this country having some kind of identity of their own. Before that, we were kind of looking to America for kind of musical tips, and political tips, too. The Black American experience is very different from that of the UK, so we naturally looked to the land of our parents, Jamaica. We were from Jamaica but we weren't Jamaican either. We were this weird, new social experiment. We were Black. And we were British, which kind of rolls off the tongue now. But trust me, back then it was a very confusing concept. And it took a very long time for it to actually mean something. I don't think it actually all came together until something like late '80s with the advent of Soul II Soul. That's when being Black and British actually meant something.[11]

Thanks to the growing demand for danceable records, the impact of Lovers Rock on the scene was such that a series of sound systems identifiable Lovers began to emerge, attracting an increasingly wider female audience. At first, Reggae purists resisted the change, but when internal impulses were joined by the arrival of Electro and Rap music from the United States, an entire generation of London soundboys embraced a new music scene.

[11] Don Letts interview: https://reggae-steady-ska.com/sweet-romance-don-letts-talks-lovers-rock.

Soul Sound System

During the 1980s, Soul sound systems began to spread, followed by Hip Hop sound systems, and thus the scene began to diversify and was no longer exclusive territory of Reggae. Some were born during that period, while others passed the torch to the next generation, who were interested in exploring new music and ways of manipulating sound and records.

Based on the continuity between toasting and rapping, Reggae and Breakbeat, the different scenes began to co-exist in multiple areas of the city. This convergence was also evident in the programming of pirate radios, Reggae nights in soul clubs and, above all, in the openness of sound systems to Soul music and the charm of new DJing styles. The social geography of the city was changing, leading to the emergence of a multiracial movement. Soul music became synonymous with these parties, with that joyful mix of whites and Blacks, men and women, all united to dance on the dancefloor.

As Derek Yates emphasises in Lloyd Bradley's *Sound Like London*:

> It was a bunch of people who weren't really Soul Train and weren't really Bob Marley, but at the same time they were all of that. Just none of it exclusively. It was how mixed up people's tastes really were in London – you could be into a bit of electro and a bit of RUN DMC, but also in Yellowman and Lovers' Rock and Parliament. [...] London had such a strong cultural feel of its own. What so many kids were really into was how things became something else when they came to London. That was what became Mastermind, became Good Times, Soul II Soul... all those new London-based

sound systems, that were very different from traditional Reggae sound systems.[12]

Norman Jay ▶ I realised it was essentially a generational thing, as the first generation of sound systems that had been set up in this country were very traditional and would only do things in the original Jamaican way [...] Now the Reggae industry in England was keeping it that way because all concerned felt comfortable with it. [...] I was part of a new generation that recognised the sound system as having the potential to be the perfect creative and commercial business model, if managed properly, but saw it as having potential far beyond Reggae dances, which hadn't evolved in 30 years. Even soul guys only ten years older than me were so set in their ways that it never occurred to them that a sound system could play funk, to them sound systems were just Reggae and that was that. My generation were asking: "Why can't we use the same methods and play James Brown instead of Dennis Brown?".[13]

Try to imagine the frustration of those young people who were looking for something that represented that strange hybrid that was their generation. Try to imagine the frustration of those looking for something different from the Reggae sound systems run by adults, just at the very moment when Punk had shown the power of the *do-it-yourself* ethos. Reggae was part of a continuum dominated by complex relationships between fathers and sons, which characterised both its Jamaican origins and its adaptation in the UK. They were not spaces for teenage experimentation, but rather sophisticated environments with

[12] Lloyd Bradley, *Sounds Like London*, Serpent Tail's, London, 2013, p. 296.
[13] Norman Jay, *Mister Good Times*, Dialogue Books, London 2019, p. 239.

an intergenerational hierarchy. While they provided a safe platform for Black expression, they also imposed significant constraints on innovation. The Rastafarian philosophy was not shared by everyone, many Black youth didn't want to be soldiers in war against Babylon. Hence the need to find other forms to represent the multiculturalism of that first generation born and raised in England. Times were changing, and when Lloyd Coxsone played those first *Lovers Rock* songs at his parties, the scene began to expand its boundaries.

Simon Jones ▶ That was the result of a kind of shift towards Black American music. There has always been an audience for American music in Black Britain but this soul sound system became popular in the early 80s with the emergence of Hip Hop culture and rap. Also, certain shifts in American soul music which took on a more political consciousness in that period. So you have this kind of generational shift away from Jamaica which was moving more in a dancehall direction, DJ oriented, slackness, away from that and towards Black America. You start to see the emergence of movements around Soul, Funk, Rare Groove, which took on some of the elements of Reggae sound system culture and used the same methods, aesthetic, technologies and applied them to a different musical content, most notably figures like Jazzie B and Norman Jay. We're not talking about a hard division between Soul and Reggae, you know Soul vs Reggae, we're talking about two parallel movements which influence each other and that tells you a lot about Black British musical culture. Soul sound systems came to prominence in the early 80s, and in many ways were modelled on the Reggae sound systems and you get the same struggles for autonomous spaces around the warehouse parties, early raves, the same kind of craft technologies, the same kind of cultural economies.

Norman Jay ▶ Sound systems started off as Reggae sound systems because they couldn't find any legal club to play Reggae. There were very few. So people created their own systems and this is the Jamaican way. Late 70s early 80s some of them started playing Soul. You had some people like soul 2 soul which at the beginning was playing Reggae but moved towards being a Soul sound or Mastermind sound system which turned into soul and then Hip Hop.[14]

Sir Drew ▶ The very first illegal raves I used to attend were heavily influenced by Soul and Funk music. These sound systems were emulating the approach taken by Reggae sound systems. You had Studio One and Saxon already hosting their "Shabeens" and illegal raves. However, other sound systems focused on Soul music started to emerge because people were deeply into Soul at that time. They would play tracks known as "Rare Grooves".

The Rare Grooves originated from Funk, Jazz and Soul records released in America between 1968 and 1975, before the arrival of Disco music. The term had been circulating among Reggae sound systems for many years identifying the oldie sessions, Soul vinyl records played at those parties. The Rare Grooves became popular in the 1980s thanks to the title of Norman Jay's Saturday afternoon radio show on Kiss FM. His approach moved away from the Reggae influences

[14] Lloyd Bradley, *Sounds Like London*, Serpent's Tail, London 2013, p. 297.

on contemporary Soul and leaned towards a rougher Funk, which made his broadcasts very appealing for a white audience as well. For instance, Maceo and The Macks' *Cross the Track*' epitomizes the infectious energy of the era, with its irresistible breakbeat, Bootsy Collins' steady bass line laying the groundwork, the brass section's powerful blasts, and those piercing keyboards. It's a track that exemplifies the sound that set the dancefloor on fire during those years.

Dizzi Heights ▶ I had my own small sound system, and I believe that was when the first Soul sounds began to make their way onto the scene. The Carnival, which was predominantly Reggae, started diversifying with a few Soul sounds, so we carved out our own space to play Soul music. While traditional Reggae sets were common in the past, we introduced a new kind of sound, featuring funk, Hip Hop, breakbeats. Additionally, we set up small arenas for breakdancers."

Imagine those young people performing Popping and Breaking steps within a cypher, the circle of dancers where the b-boys showcased their skills. Up until that point, at Reggae sound system parties, you would see circles where *Skank* was the dance style. However, with the change in music selection, there was an inevitable transformation in dance styles and moves. *Skank* originated in the 1950s and 1960s in Jamaica with the rise of Ska music. When this music became popular among English mods and skinheads, Skank also spread contextually. The style came back into fashion between the 1970s and 1980s thanks to the *2-tone* movement. With the arrival of Electro and Hip Hop music the dances became more spectacular.

Norman Jay ▶ It was the breakthrough of Lovers' rock sounds that opened everybody's eyes to the real entertainment prospects of the sound systems, and things started to get more refined. Lloyd Coxsone was on the cusp of that new generation, because sounds of that era had a whole different energy to the ones that went before. They weren't like the yardie-style sounds, they were more about us in London – more fish and chips than rice and peas! Then we wanted to take it up a bit more. Lover's rock made the dance more sophisticated and we, Norman and Paul Anderson (Trouble Funk Sound System) and Mastermind took it on from there. We acted like Reggae sound systems, so we had all that heritage and attention to detail, but we were banging James Brown.[15]

James McNally ▶ Mastermind started as a Reggae sound system, but in the early '80s, they switched over to being a soul sound system, renaming themselves Mastermind Road Show. They were introduced to cassettes of New York dance music DJs and various post-disco street Funk styles, which strongly influenced them to experiment with mixing techniques, creating imaginative blends of different music genres.

Dizzi Heights ▶ A typical Reggae sound system primarily consists of bass bins and employs a single turntable for the DJ to play from. In contrast, Mastermind used multiple turntables. They predominantly featured all-American imports, with only a few British selections.

---

[15] Lloyd Bradley, *Sounds Like London*, Serpent's Tail, London 2013, p. 302.

Mastermind Roadshow at the Hippodrome in 1985 (credits Martin Jones)

The crew itself was quite diverse, comprising both black and white members.

Bunny Bread ▶ Mastermind came through having a Reggae sound system. So they make that transition now using that same Hip Hop sensibility: cutting, scratching, you know, mixing in a certain manner. They held significant influence in the early use of two turntables and manipulation.

Dave VJ ▶ As Mastermind we played probably only 3 years all over the place, but our biggest thing was the carnival. We became legendary at carnival, because everybody else in that period who had a soul sound had a very tiny sound. You know, the sound was rubbish. So Herbie, what they did was get the same sound that was playing Reggae, because Reggae was very heavy, and played Soul. Anybody that came anywhere near was just blown away, and that was how we made a name for ourselves.

THE NOTTING HILL CARNIVAL

Notting Hill Carnival, a music festival that takes place every year on the last weekend of August, attracting over a million people to Northwest London, around the Portobello area.

It originated from the fusion of two Caribbean-inspired events: a carnival celebration organised by Trinidadian activist Claudia Jones for the first time in 1959, as a direct response to the racial tensions in the area and the racist murder of Kelso Cochrane, and the street festival organised by Rhaune Laslett. In the late 1960s, these events coalesced into what would evolve into the modern carnival, featuring decorated floats accompanied by dancers and musicians, many of whom played steel drums, known as steel pans. These improvised percussion instruments were originally crafted from oil barrels and have their roots in Trinidad.

In the early 1970s, the carnival expanded with the increasing participation of activists who organised folkloric and music competitions, consequently transforming into the most significant

Notting Hill Carnival, London 2013

cultural celebration of London's Black community. In 1975, under the presidency of Leslie "*Teacher*" Palmer, who worked for Chris Blackwell's *Island Records*, Reggae music played from the sound systems scattered along the carnival route became dominant, replacing the Steel bands and Calypso. This happened as Reggae was entering its most militant phase, giving the festival an increasingly political connotation. Palmer had the support of local radio stations like *London* and *Capital* to promote the 1975 edition, which saw the participation of over half a million people.

In the 1980s, Soul and Funk were first introduced as genres to the carnival thanks to Norman Jay and his sound system, *Good Times*. It was a courageous move and not accepted by everyone at first, but it paved the way for other Soul sounds like *Rampage*, *Rapattack* etc. At that moment, the carnival soundtrack began to expand its sounds to include Rap music.

Norman Jay ▶ I think the most significant moment was when we turned the decks around. All Reggae sounds will work with their desk against the wall, usually in a corner, so they've got to play their sound with the back to the crowd, to protect their equipment and so nobody could see the records they are playing. [...]. We started off like that because that was what we knew, then we turned them around so we faced the crowd and we could all be part of the same experience – inclusive. Considerably more important than inclusiveness in itself was the fact that it was being driven from a Black perspective.[16]

Dizzi Heights ▶ What Hip Hop introduced was the crossfader, which allowed DJs to go beyond simply playing

[16] Lloyd Bradley, *Sounds Like London*, Serpent's Tail, London 2013, pp. 302-303.

Wall of speakers at Notting Hill Carnival, 2013

one track and then another. With a crossfader, you could have both tracks playing simultaneously and mix between them. While our equipment consisted of 1200s, Stanton turntables, and a mixer, Reggae sound systems typically used 1200s, a powerful preamp, a substantial amplifier, along with 18 to 24 speakers, large bass bins, and some mid-range and high-frequency speakers. We, on the other hand, preferred a setup with two 1200s and aimed for more balanced sound, incorporating mid-range and high-frequency elements alongside the bass. This approach allowed us to craft a distinctive sound, marking the beginning of our unique musical style.

Ishmahil Blagrove ▶ The emergence of Hip Hop and scratching marked a shift toward more complex equipment. In the earlier days, the setup was less technical, and even the speaker boxes were simple square designs with treble coming out of them. The complexity increased with technological advancements. While Soul sound systems could be arranged much like Reggae systems, with two turntables, an amplifier, and speakers, the advent of Hip Hop introduced a new level of interaction with the equipment. DJs began to physically manipulate the turntables, touching the record while it was playing, going beyond simply playing a dubplate. They would stop the record, cut in another section, and even play two copies of the same track simultaneously. This required a different set of skills and artistry to master.

In the 1980s, in addition to the pioneering sound of *Mastermind Roadshow*, two Soul sound systems and two selectors, made their mark on the scene: Norman Jay and Jazzie B. Both represented the aspirations of a generation of Londoners who wanted something more from the city they were born into.

Norman Jay, son of immigrants from Grenada, grew up in the highly concentrated Black area of Notting Hill. His father had an extensive collection of Black music records, and like in many Caribbean families, the Blaupunkt "*Blue Spo*t" radio was proudly placed in the centre of the living room. The music genres played initially were Jazz and Rhythm & Blues and later, from the mid-1960s, Jamaican music like Bluebeat, Ska and Rocksteady. Although Jay loved Reggae, he was more interested in Soul music, and in his imagination, he didn't envision Kingston but rather the entertainment venues of the

English working class of that time: the stadium, Soul clubs and the Soho neighbourhood. His younger brother Joey was passionate about electronics, so they built their sound system, *Great Tribulation*, together, using cabinets and reclaimed wood.

Joey grew his dreadlocks and found his place in the Reggae scene, while Norman wanted something different. He regularly visited New York because a large part of his relatives lived there, during one of these trips in 1979, he discovered that his uncle ran the city's largest sound system. Shortly after he attended his first block party, where he witnessed the birth of Hip Hop. In 1982, Joey and Norman renamed their sound system *Good Times*, signifying not only a change in name but also a change in sound. Their strong point was an eclectic mix of new and old sounds.

In the same year, Jay began a collaboration with the Notting Hill Carnival, breaking any unwritten rules playing Soul, Funk and Disco music in what had always been the realm of Reggae. His eclectic sets attracted an increasingly multiracial crowd, prompting him to move to Southern Row, towards the northern border of the carnival, in search of larger spaces to make his audience dance. Combining the aesthetics of Mods with the DIY ethos of Punk and sound systems and blending it all with his collection of American Soul and Funk records, Jay conquered the entire West area of London.

Something very similar was happening in the northern neighbourhoods of the city. Trevor Beresford Romeo, son of immigrants from Antigua, had built his first sound system called Jah Rico as a teenager. Taking advantage of the carpentry lessons he attended at school, Romeo and his friends-built speakers that they transported around the city with a shopping cart, since they were too young to drive vehicles. After graduating, Romeo obtained a job as a sound engineer

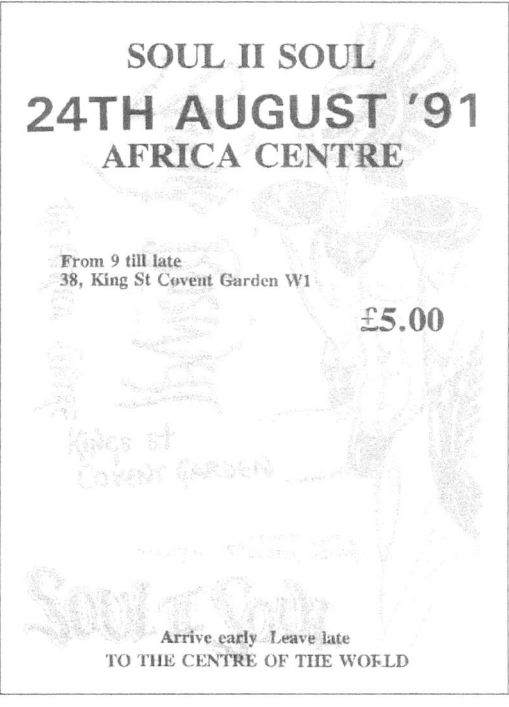

SOUL II SOUL

24TH AUGUST '91

AFRICA CENTRE

From 9 till late
38, King St Covent Garden W1

£5.00

Arrive early Leave late
TO THE CENTRE OF THE WORLD

Flyer for a Soul II
Soul Party at the
Africa Center

in a studio, helping the singer and dancer Tommy Steele, who taught him the fundamentals of sound design, recording and dubplate cutting. During that time, he also started another business: a clothes and record stall in *Camden Market*.

Romeo, with Jah Rico, mainly played Reggae, but when he heard the new sounds coming from the United States like Electro, Soul and Hip Hop, he decided to change his name to Jazzie B, and his sound system formed by Jazzie Q, Aitch B, Daddae Harvey, was renamed *Soul II Soul*. They were the ones who coined the term *Funki Dred* to describe that British variant of militant Afrocentrism that was emerging in American Rap music at the time, devoid of separatist and conflictual aspects. The proposition of *Soul II Soul* oscillated between a utopian ideal and the desire for integration, with a more commercial perspective that seemed to best define the emerging Black British culture. For every love song and expression of optimism, there were others that solicited pride, unity and self-determination.

The combination of Rare Grooves, Rap and Electro music created a dialogue between 1980s Great Britain and 1970s America, both grappling with the same social and political contradictions. As the audience at those parties grooved to the beats of *Soul Power '74* by Maceo Parker, which sampled Martin Luther King's "I Have a Dream" speech, or to Keith LeBlanc's electronic reimagining of Malcolm X's "No Sell Out" speech, it felt like the divide was narrowing. The aspiration for freedom that once fuelled the civil rights and Black power movements was now being harnessed to address the challenges of London's reality. For young Black and White people, this music was a sort of crash course on Black art and politics.[17]

---

[17] Caspar Melville, *It's a London Thing: How Rare Groove, Acid House*

From Reggae to Hip Hop

MC Mello ▶ When it comes to the Reggae sound systems, the toasters, the MCs, and the chatters were perfectionists, and they inspired generations to write and get involved. When Hip Hop culture came along, we already had schooling through Reggae sound systems. We had a foundation that merged, matched, and went hand in hand with Hip Hop. They were coming from the same place, the same grassroots, the same types of people, the same experiences, the same laws and rules, bass lines, beats, rhythms, rhymes, and words. But different regions, different countries, different societies, yet the same energy, the same blood.

Rodney P ▶ Now, within Hip Hop and Reggae, there are some real similarities. I guess you could say that Kool Herc, who came from Jamaica to America, brought the Reggae sensibility with him to the United States. So, you could argue that Hip Hop is as much a Jamaican art form as it is an American art form.

Norman Jay ▶ It was a Caribbean thing and all that was different was the soundtrack. The battling, the running down of opponents, the off-the-cut wit was exactly the same – we called it toasting, they called it rapping.[18]

Thanks to the strong presence of Jamaican immigrants in

and Jungle Remapped the City, Manchester University Press, Manchester 2019, p. 249.

[18] Norman Jay, *Mister Good Times*, Dialogue Books, London 2019, pp 191-192.

the suburbs of New York, different cultural forms associated with the Reggae scene were incorporated into the emerging Hip Hop culture. For example, Kool Herc, together with his friend Coke La Rock, managed to create an original style, drawing inspiration from some Kingston DJs like Count Machuki, U-Roy and Big Youth.

It was Kool Herc himself who developed technological adaptations, especially in terms of amplification power and speaker sizes, as well as improved separation of sound frequencies. Reggae and Hip Hop music relied on the manipulation of vinyl records and their transformation into something new during the live shows. The most important technique was mixing, which emerged from the need to maintain a continuous musical flow between songs, allowing the audience to dance without interruptions. The song's selection was an element of primary importance in the DJ set, as the choice of songs and the order in which they were played determined a DJ's popularity. Through his selections, DJs aimed to establish a shared dialogue, taking the audience on an adventurous sonic journey and igniting people's energy on the dancefloor.

Also Toasting and Rapping are two common elements of enormous importance. The use of the microphone enriched the musical selection through vocal improvisation. Dubbing allowed Reggae DJs to express with orality on instrumental versions of songs through Toasting, the precursor to MCing. With the arrival on the scene of a selector like King Tubby, a new standard emphasised bass and rhythm, enabling U-Roy to deliver mind-boggling Toasting performances. It was in the live experience, at local parties, at home, in talent shows or jam sessions that Toasters and later Rappers found spaces for discussions, refining, and competing with others' skills.

The Jamaican slang mixed with the London dialect, gave rise to a new language used to create a sense of inclusivity and community. Linguistic and narrative boundaries were transcended, offering a stark contrast to the racial divisions present in British society. Moreover, these were all inclusive parties, often shared spaces with other social groups, particularly young white working-class people, especially in the outskirts of big cities.

For this reason, both Reggae and Hip Hop adapted in a very unique way in the UK, transforming those dancefloors into spaces of solidarity, survival, and identity affirmation for those who shared the same conditions of marginalisation.

Simon Jones ▶ You can see the legacy of sound system culture in British Hip Hop culture. You can see it in the orality, the methodologies, the performance practices, all division of labour in the Hip Hop crew around Hip Hop sound systems, the democratic character of Rap, the modes of expressions, those owes so much to Reggae sound systems' DJing and toasting, the whole aesthetic of riding a rhythm, the aesthetic of spontaneity, live spontaneity. The parallel between Reggae and Hip Hop orality is very clear.

Linton Lee ▶ The Sound System culture was crucial for Hip Hop culture. Many of the Hip Hop artists who are still active today from the early days probably had connections to sound systems. They might have owned sound systems themselves, been involved in engineering, wiring, or had relatives in the sound system scene, as it was a community affair. Your friends would be at the sound clashes or sound system parties, and it was a neighborhood thing. However, the younger generation, while looking up to sound systems, sought something different. They harbored a lot of creativity in the forms of dance, graffiti art, rap, and musicianship, aspects that the sound systems weren't fully addressing. While sound systems were great for bringing the community together to enjoy music, we began to realize that we could meld our music with the Reggae influence and create our own distinct scene.

Bunny Bread ▶ So, when we examine sound system culture, which played an integral role in our growth and contributed to the development of Hip Hop culture, we find that we already had that competitive mindset ingrained in our DNA. By the time Hip Hop emerged, we were already ready for it.

Sparkii Ski ▶ The English scene came up with sound system culture which to this day I believe it's the foundation of Hip Hop. I don't recognize Hip Hop as being a NYC art form, I consider it to be a Jamaican sound system art form. Being the bass, the dj, the battling, the selecting, the rhythms, the remixes, the versioning culture, all this stuff I've always considered to be of Jamaican lineage. In the UK there's a large amount of Black people being Caribbean or directly Jamaican. I'm the first of my family to be born in England. I think there's a direct connection with sound system culture.

Rodney P ▶ Sound System culture in England was enormous then. In my opinion, the best UK MCs are the ones who started their career doing Reggae, because they had a clear understanding of the vibes, and how to roll up, and how to control an audience. Hip Hop came as an after flow. And it was a thing where the style of MCing was different. But it was something that we knew how to deal with, you know.

E=mix ▶ To transition from Reggae to Hip Hop was quite a challenge because you become set in your ways. However, when Hip Hop actually emerged, it was distinct and it began to inspire us in a different manner. Consequently, things began to take shape. I would say we were influenced by the Reggae side, and we would incorporate a technique known as Sing Jay. We might not necessarily be rapping, but we adopted a different flow and style.

The appeal of Rap music lies in its ability to mix various musical genres to create something new. As Hip Hop became increasingly popular worldwide, a sort of dilemma began to arise for those outside the United States. A gap opened between those who wanted to remain tied to the origins of the Bronx and those who sought to express their own identity, modifying it based on their present-day local experiences.

As music writer Andy Wood points out:

For those in Anglophone countries, however, asserting their own identity onto the music is not so simple. Within London, the choice to speak "your lingo" meant that the music was more locally grounded and maintained a distinct self, separate from those rappers coming from the US.[19].

[19] Andy Wood, *London Posse and the Birth of British Hip Hop*, "Atlantic Studies", 6, 2009, pp. 175-190.

london
posse

UK Style

Black British Culture

In the English scene there have been several attempts to shape musical genres and subgenres that originated within the African or Asian diaspora, adapting them to British reality in an original and innovative way. The same happened with Hip Hop culture. Musical genres born in the former Caribbean colonies or on American soil have been interpreted and re-elaborated in forms that can be radically different as well.

Historian Stuart Hall has emphasised this trend in his writings by describing the transition from a generation that reproduced Caribbean culture to a new one aimed to leave their own mark, "from an Afro-Caribbean presence in Great Britain to the emergence of a Black British culture". For those young people, it was easy to identify with London rather than with Jamaica, which they only knew indirectly from their parents' stories. It is precisely at that moment that an original identity begins to develop.

In the early 1970s, they no longer felt out of place, or lacking because they were neither Caribbean nor English. Thus, a new generation was born, different from the previous ones. It was for this reason that music, poetry, literature and the language used told the story of this collective experience, characterised by transformation, anxiety, challenge and hope. Their politics were expressed through music, or perhaps music itself had become a vehicle of their political opinions.

We are facing a complex generational transition. Until that moment, the lives of adults were heavily racialized, with Caribbean migrants keeping England out of their own home and meeting places. However, the younger generation, born later, had to negotiate their relationship with the surrounding environment in a very different way.

As Paul Gilroy emphasised:

I think it's an extraordinary period, because what you have in that time is an extraordinary cultural, political, historical energy coming out of the Caribbean. You have a greater wave of energy coming out of America, in the aftermath of the Black Power period, telling the world, actually, that Black was beautiful; telling the world that the history and culture of African Americans was, or could be, a planetary resource, a resource for anybody who wanted to make use of it and encounter its pleasures. And, at the same time, you have a kind of demographic wave in the big cities here, where young people are looking around for the elements of a Black culture that they are going to create and negotiate, but they know it can't be a Caribbean culture, and they know it can't be an African American culture, although they draw elements of both and combine them in different ways. And finally – I mean this is a long period – in the mid 80s, probably a 20 years cycle of cultural life, they reach a period where they no longer imitate, no longer simply mimic things born elsewhere, but feel confident and comfortable in a culture that they've improvised for themselves, from far flung elements but also out of the texture of their own immediate experience.[1]

BLACK PANTHER MOVEMENT

The history of the Black Panther Movement in London dates back to the mid-1960s, when a group of Black militants began attending *Speakers' Corner* in Hyde Park. Among them there was the Nigerian playwright Obi Egbuna, Dominican activist Eddie LeCointe, the Nigerian Sam Saagay, the Guyanese orator Roy Sawh, and Trinidadian Michael X, essentially the founding core of that movement. *Speakers' Corner* quickly became a platform for the dissemination of Black nationalism and Pan-Africanism. This group of friends was an eclectic mix of radical figures, all coming from previous experiences of struggle.

While the international attention was completely focused on the escalating war in Vietnam and the expanding liberation struggles worldwide, an event/meeting titled *Dialectics of Liberation* was organised in July 1967, bringing together academics and activists. Intellectuals and writers like Herbert Marcuse, Allen Ginsberg and Joseph Berke participated in the event, held at the *Camden Roundhouse* in North London, a popular haunt for the militant scene of that time. The main orator was

[1] Interview with Paul Gilroy in Mike and Charlie Phillips, *Windrush: The Irresistible Rise of Multi-Racial Britain*, Harpers Collins, London 1998, pp. 285-286.

the African-American activist Stokely Carmichael, who urged the Black brothers in England to create a militant front inspired by the Black Power philosophy, as theorised in the United States, to oppose the racist policies of the British establishment.

Riding the emotional wave of that meeting, the English *Black Power Movement* began to structure itself. The organisations born in the aftermath of that speech adopted radical positions from the outset against capitalism, racism and colonialism and advocated the principle of self-defence, even through the use of force if necessary. Among these groups were the *Black Liberation Front*, the *Black Unity and Freedom Party* and the *Racial Adjustment Action Society*. Unlike the preceding groups, the Black Power Movement formed grassroots collectives with a strong presence in the poorest and more densely areas populated by the Black community.

Obi Egbuna was elected president of the *Universal Coloured People's Association* and a manifesto titled *Black Power in Britain* was published, proposing a philosophy aligned with the most radical groups of the US scene. In 1968, after a trip to the USA, Egbuna resigned from his role as president and founded the *Black Panther Movement* (*BPM*).

The group drew direct inspiration directly from the politics and imagery of the Black Panthers in America. Egbuna intended to organize the group as a covert revolutionary underground organization, but he was unable to implement his ideas as he was arrested on charges of alleged incitement to violence against the police, stemming from a pamphlet he authored and titled *What to Do if Cops Lay Their Hands on Black Man at Speakers' Corner*. In the text, he advocated self-defence by any means necessary: "The moment the cops lay their hands on a Black brother, it is the duty of [the] Black crowd [to] surge forward like one big Black steam roller to catch up with the cop... till the brother is rescued, freed and made to flee at once".

At that time, Altheia Jones, Eddie LeCointe, Farrukh Dhondy and Neil Kenlock took the reins of the group by shifting its strategic focus towards grassroots struggles such as combating workplace discrimination and housing allocation and proposing alternative solutions in the fields of education and healthcare. Under Jones' leadership, the English Panthers became a highly effective community organisation. While mainstream media depicted BPM as a group of violent extremists, white counterculture magazines like *OZ*, *International Times* and *INK* supported the Panther's anti-authoritarian politics. The group also published a newsletter, the *Black People's News Service*, and later the *Freedom News* magazine.

At the beginning of the 1970s, the group had about 3000 members, mostly based in Notting Hill and Brixton, and they also opened branches in major English cities. The peak of their public visibility came during the 1970's trial of the *Mangrove Nine*, a group of BPM supporters, including Altheia Jones, Darcus Howe and Barbara Beese. The group was charged with incitement to riot during a demonstration against the ongoing police raids on the *Mangrove Restaurant* in Ladbroke Grove, a very popular meeting place for the Caribbean community. During the trial, the defendants captured the public attention, by demanding to be judged by an all-Black jury and the courageous decision of three militants to defend themselves without any lawyer. The bold defence strategy, the support from countercultural publications, and solidarity extended by Black organisations, led to their acquittal on the most serious charges.

For the first time, a judge publicly acknowledged the existence of clear instances of widespread racial hatred within the London police force.

The experience of the BPM came to an end after a few years, in 1973, when the party split into factions and separate formations.

Observing this change, Henry Louis Gates wrote in his essay *A Reporter at Large*:

They turned marginality into a very creative art form – life form really – and they've done so at a level of youth culture, music, dress... They styled their way into the British Culture.[2]

Expanding on this concept, Stuart Hall states that:

Young people began to identify themselves by their experience in Britain, rather than in terms of how they felt about themselves in the Caribbean. It was the beginning of the development of a distinctive Black British identity, prior to which growing up in Britain had meant that you lacked some elements of authenticity as a Caribbean. At the beginning of the seventies that began to change, and it became a major characteristic of the new generation which began to understand itself as being uniquely different. Its politics became its cultural expression, or perhaps vice versa, its cultural expression became its politics. The music, the poetry, the language all spoke of the shared experience of transformation and anxiety and defiance and hope. Young Black British style became the same as the content of their protest. Both reflected the same complexity, the same fragmentation, the same movement, the same disturbance.[3]

That's exactly what happened: excluded from West End clubs or suburban nightclubs, the Black music scene became autonomous, DIY, outlawed, community-driven, and increasingly innovative. Following the internal dynamics, microeconomy, and the sensibility of the previous generation's Blues party, the sound systems of the 1980s found themselves interacting with the new sophisticated and cosmopolitan Black

[2] Henry Louis Gates Jr., *A Reporter at Large*, in Kwesi Owusu (a c. di), *Black British Culture & Society. A Text Reader*, Routledge, London-New York 2000.
[3] Mike e Trevor Phillips, *Windrush*, cit., pp. 273-274.

London. Many DJs and MCs, who had grown up in local sound systems, made contributions to the scene, all while being drawn to the allure of the city where they were born.

That invisible wall of racism that forced people to stay within their own spaces, far away from the places of English culture, was being dismantled. Not wanting to accept any form of second-class citizenship and armed with the tools that their parents lacked, this generation was brave and uncompromising, just like music that began to define new forms of self-determination.

Fast Chat

Fast Chat, just like *Lovers Rock*, was one of the earliest and most significant innovations in the local scene, representing a profound change from the orthodox Reggae coming from Jamaica. The productions consisted of minimalist versions of Dancehall songs, featuring lyrics inspired by real-life experiences in the streets of UK cities. These songs were unmistakably designed to make people dance, all while still allowing space for messages of protest. *Fast Chat* was rhythmically captivating, to the point that several tracks became hits and even entered the charts. The pioneers of this style were the DJs (Toasters) of a South London sound system: *Saxon International Sound*.

Created in 1976 by Lloyd Francis and Dennis Rowe, it was considered one of the best in the United Kingdom in the 1980s.

Tippa Irie ▶ In those days, I began winning talent competitions, and it was during one of these competitions that

147

Tippa Irie, october 2021 (credits Nicola Cavalazzi)

Dennis Rowe and Lloyd Francis, the owners of Saxon Sound, spotted me. They were in the process of recruiting talent for their sound system. So they said to me, "Hey, we'll give you 10 pounds if you come and DJ with us". Cecil Tubbys was only paying me three pounds. I thought these guys had a bit more resources since they were hustling, so I decided to check them out. When I went to their place, I found Maxi Priest, Papa Levi, Daddy Colonel, and other incredibly talented individuals. We all shared a common passion: music. I was inspired to give it my all. When you're performing alongside such talent, you want to match or even surpass their skills. So, when you grab the microphone, you make sure you're fully prepared and deliver your best.

Fast Chat was actually created by Peter King in 1982, but it was Smiley Culture, Tippa Irie and Papa Levi who recorded tracks like *Cockney Translation*, *Hello Darling* and

Mi God, Mi King which entered the UK top 40 between 1983 and 1985.

Tippa Irie ▶ Most of the MCing styles at the time were pretty laid back. However, there was this guy named Peter King who came up with a fast style. Back in the day, when we used to spar, whenever someone created something new, whether it was me, Levi, Peter King, or anyone else, we'd all borrow it and put our own twist on it. So when Peter introduced this fast style and started performing it, everyone was like, "Yeah, that's it!" and we all adopted it. That's when Levi wrote *My God My King*, with his fast-chat style: "Jah man mi cool, nuh stubborn like mule". Then I came up with "All the time the lyrics a rhyme", Daddy Colonel had "How do you roll your tongue, Daddy Colonel", and Smiley Culture contributed "Slam bam, Jah man, come hear dem fashion". Everyone crafted their own versions, and from that point on, we collectively transformed the landscape of Reggae music in England.

Fast Chat was a departure from traditional Reggae, characterised by powerful bass lines and drum beats, which were replaced with a mix of synths and drum machines. Diverging from the classic *Toasting* tradition as well, the DJs of the Saxon sound system wrote lyrics that progressively became more complex and rapped them with an increasingly fast flow. Most importantly, they narrated their everyday experiences in the streets of London without any reference to Jamaica and Rastafarian themes.

Furthermore, they expressed themselves in a sort of mix between Cockney and Patois, alternating between the two

slangs even between the same song. As Tippa Irie explains, "When you are at home with your parents, you speak Patois, but when you are with your friend Tom from Stratford or East Ham, you speak like him". Although this duality was a daily practice, it was only with Fast Chat that it made its debut on record in one of the first Black musical productions capable of incorporating the contradictions of British society, while also attempting to redefine it.

Tippa Irie ▶ That was definitely the first recognisable UK dancehall style. You had Yellowman, Peter Metro and all these people hearing our sound tapes and chatting about our lyrics back in Jamaica. So we changed it around and they were influenced by us for a change. Of course the people in Jamaica didn't know about us, so those guys would chat our lyrics in the dance and make people believe they created them. Mainly, Reggae culture in this country is looking to Jamaica the whole time – that's a really interesting moment where that pattern is reversed and England influences what's going on in Jamaica. We created phrases like "Lickwood" [in response to a big tune] and stuff like that in our dances. Then you'd hear Johnny Osbourne and Junior Reid and people like that singing our styles and using our terminology. So that was unique because everybody was focused on Jamaica at the time. We came and changed it and sped it up a little and then we kind of inspired people like Papa San, Lieutenant Stitchie and Professor Nuts and all these people.

The adaptation of Jamaican music to the needs of Black youth indicated how Black British culture was in the process of definition. As historian Michael La Rose wrote: "There was a change underway. The young people no longer defined themselves as Caribbean but began to identify themselves as Black British. This new style reflected that evolution by narrating British experiences".

As the writer Adebayo stated in a 2011 article in "The Guardian": *Artists like Smiley Cultures have made speaking in Cockney cool.* The creation of Fast Chat marked a new phase of that development.

Tippa Irie ▶ Who was known for fast chatting during that period? The sound tapes had a way of resonating with people in a manner that Black music in the UK hadn't managed until then. It was because they heard their own

Cover of the single 'Cockney Translation' by Smiley Culture, 1984

experiences and voices reflected in those tapes. You see, we essentially grew up in London, and naturally, we talked about what we witnessed in London. We aimed to distinguish ourselves from Jamaican artists. People used to compete over who had the best tape, who had the most powerful lyrics on their tape, and which MC reigned supreme. During that time, MCs and sound tapes became central in our lives. We created something that people could relate to because we were rapping about things they saw daily, the experiences that we, as Black people living in Britain, were going through. The Brixton riots, for example, were among the topics we addressed. It was like reading the newspaper when you came to one of our dances, particularly when listening to artists like Macka B and Papa Levi. Their lyrics were forthright, they told it like it was. I chatted in a similar vein, but with a slightly less militant and a more approachable tone.

Simon Jones ▶ You need to consider the specific stylistic shift that accompanied the rise of fast-style DJing and the transformation of themes and content in DJ lyrics. This marked the emergence of a distinct Black British DJing style. While there were certainly influences from Jamaican DJs, a new generation of British DJs embraced these influences and developed highly innovative styles. They seamlessly blended patois with regional working-class accents, combined Black British vernacular with Cockney rhyming slang, as seen in tracks like *Cockney Translation* and *Police Officer* by Smiley Culture.

In 1984, Smiley Culture released *Cockney Translation* on *Fashion Label*. The record touched the soul of the fans and reached the top of the British Reggae charts, remaining there for several weeks. Like many young Black people of his generation, Smiley Culture was exploring new musical frontiers. The Saxon DJ played with slangs, Cockney and Patois, and with identities, Cockney, meaning English, and Yardy, meaning Jamaican. In that song, Smiley seems to be two distinct people. Although he is a Londoner, he is a Black Londoner. He is not a white working-class person, but not even a Jamaican. He can speak both languages, but neither truly belongs to him.

On the cover of the twelve-inch record, there is a picture of him leaning against a car parked on a typical South London street. Smiley wears a cap, a sheepskin coat, and several jewels, with a ring for each finger of the left hand and two gold chains around his neck. The cover seems like an advertisement that evokes more the image of a car salesman. However, Smiley plays with words, accents and even clothing, reflecting on issues of identity and Black culture.

Adebayo recalls, "I was at a Saxon Sound party when I heard Smiley Culture sing his Cockney anthem. And you know, for the first time in my life, I understood what it meant being Black and British... and I was proud of it. And I wasn't the only one. I saw that same reaction in the over five hundred young people gathered in that place".

In the track *Police Officer*, Smiley Culture addresses the issue of police harassment against Black drivers. In the recounted episode, an Afro-Caribbean artist was instructed to report to the police station within twenty-four hours after being stopped, in order to provide his driver's license and other documents that he didn't have on him during the inspection. When the young man goes to the police station, the policeman recognizes him and he asks for an autograph. The choice to use Cockney and Patois instead of standard English is significant as it aligns with the tradition of Reggae sound systems as a language of resistance against the racism of those in positions of power. Following the success of *Police Officer*, Tippa Irie's *Complain Neighbour* also became very popular.

Tippa Irie ▶ The song *Complain Neighbour*, which is one of my tracks, gained popularity due to the unique context of what was happening at that time, much like Smiley Culture's *Police Officer*. Both songs touched on the clash between our culture and the native English culture. In *Complain Neighbour*, I share a personal experience. I was at the house of a girl I knew, and we were playing music and dancing. Her baby was in the living room, and then a neighbour threw a brick through the window. All you could hear was him shouting, "Turn that damn music down", and then he ran off. This incident got me thinking, and it inspired me to write *Complain Neighbour*.

The song reflects the tension between a Jamaican family and its white neighbours who doesn't appreciate Reggae, doesn't like Black people, and wishes they weren't living next door. But, true to my style, I approached it with a more subtle tone.

The change of rhythm and speed, as well as the language used in these songs, had an impact that went far beyond the popularity of the genre; in fact, Fast Chat was also significant for the evolution of Rap music. Many pioneers of the UK Hip Hop scene, like Rodney P and Roots Manuva, still mention today the Saxon Sound as one of their main sources of inspiration. And even Adebayo himself, in his obituary for Smiley Culture, wrote: "If Smiley Culture hadn't made it cool to sing in slang, British rappers would probably still be rapping with a Yankee accent, there wouldn't be no English cadence in Drum & Bass, 2 Step, Dubstep or Grime. There would be no Dizzee or Tinie Tempah".

James McNally ▶ One of the remarkable things that occurred was that around the same time *Buffalo Gals* was released, the London Reggae scene witnessed a revolutionary development known today as the "fast style". This breakthrough took place in 1982 when a man named Peter King, who served as one of the MCs on the Saxon sound system, introduced this innovative style. It involved dancing around the rhythm, creating the illusion that it was moving twice as fast as the beat. This style quickly gained popularity in the London Reggae MC scene. If you listen to the records they were playing during that period, you'd hear them addressing important issues, essentially nation-building, and portraying the experiences of being a

Black Londoner. The close proximity of these two cultures led to people immediately embracing the fast style within Hip Hop. For instance, in the case of Family Quest's *Outer Space Rap*, listen to Cheeko's verse; he's delivering a fast style flow with a rhythmic pattern like "da da da-da-da da da". This is the Reggae fast style adapted within the context of a Rap record.

The Birth of UK Rap

For most of the audience and insiders, it was simply a variant of American Hip Hop declined through different English specificities. There was also a transnational theme, often in the background, but destined to become increasingly explicit over the years: the reunion of the African diaspora. In fact, few places like the UK demonstrated such an ability to absorb, connect, and simultaneously process Caribbean, African American and African influences, and then powerfully penetrate different contexts and the global mainstream scene. This was also because the United Kingdom, with London leading the way, was perhaps the first country in the world to distinctly reinterpret the Hip Hop formula coming from across the Atlantic.

MC Mello ▶ If you look at the music scene in London, you will find every style of music from all over the world. You'll find every club representing all the different styles, and everybody is going and tasting all these different styles and different cultures and expressions through music. London is a melting pot, not only of music and musical genres, but of cultures, languages, fashion, identities,

MC Mello, London 2012

beliefs, all of this... And what's key is that we, as Londoners, are soaking it all up.

The hybrid nature of this music contributed to the development of unique soundscapes. Not only Reggae, but also American Funk and Soul were remixed in an original way to create a distinctly British Hip Hop version. Hip Hop had the merit of introducing young people to fundamental classics, mostly unknown but useful for reconfiguring the scene of the time. The fact that these productions assembled samples of old tracks, mixing them with the most modern technology, unleashed the creativity of British beatmakers.

MC Duke ▶ London is a machine that consistently generates new music flavors; it never remains stagnant.

We altered Hip Hop by adjusting its speed and infusing our own influences, like samples and breaks, as well as music we enjoyed in the club. We didn't limit ourselves to the American preferences; we incorporated elements specific to the London scene. In the early days, everyone was primarily using James Brown samples, but we also had a scene called Rare Groove, and when we embraced Hip Hop, we incorporated tracks from that scene. This made our Hip Hop distinct from the American Hip Hop, which tended to be slower. Our culture was all about partying and dancing.

DJ Devastate ▶ Our sound was distinct because our parents hailed from the Caribbean, so we had that influence in our minds. We grew up in Tottenham, representing the first generation raised in the UK, so our influences were unique, even though we were objectively influenced by NYC Hip Hop. These influences became a part of who we were.

Sparkii Ski ▶ In the UK, the Caribbean influence is significant, with a deep love for bass frequencies and the art of controlling and hitting those frequencies. Growing up among DJs like Pogo and Custmaster Swift, I've always admired Hip Hop as a DJ culture. I have a strong affinity for breaks and breakbeat DJs. I used to attend Jams even before Hip Hop records, when a Hip Hop Jam consisted of an MC and a DJ cutting breaks. As a producer and beatmaker, part of my role is to recreate what DJs did with breaks and music, fusing them into my productions by blending various layers and sounds.

DJ Devastate ▶ Looking back now, our Reggae background subconsciously influenced us when it came to making music in the studio. Even when I was attempting to create Hip Hop music, there was an underlying Reggae tone to it. I didn't set out to make Reggae Hip Hop; it just naturally emerged because that's the music I grew up with. My parents came from the Caribbean, and my dad collected old Ska and Reggae records. It felt right because I had experience DJing in front of audiences on sound systems in a raw environment, and I had confidence in my ability to make people dance and evoke emotions. It was rooted in my experiences with sound system culture. I remember being in school, around eleven or thirteen, and going to Saxon. We were into sound system culture. We saw Tippa Irie, Papa Levi, Sandy Rusty, and years later, we would be DJing on sound systems. It's a part of us. In the studio, we carried all those experiences, energies, and vibes, infusing them into our music.

Dizzi Heights ▶ We never felt like we were imitating Rap; we saw Rap as something that showed us what we could do ourselves. While we learned from how they scratched, which provided a good starting point for us, we began to explore what sounded great to our ears. We developed our own unique scratching style and started rapping in our distinctive way.

DJ Supreme ▶ During those early days, much of our inspiration and ideas were directly imported from the US. We were in the nascent stages of the scene, so we absorbed a lot of what we learned from the US. In the beginning, there wasn't as much innovation, but there were numerous highly skilled DJs honing their craft, learning from the American style, and subsequently evolving it.

From the pioneering DJs of the scene like Cosmic Jam and Imperial Mixer, to the turntablism masters like DJ Fingers, Cutmaster Swift, DJ Supreme, DJ Pogo, DJ Devastate, and more, Great Britain was at the forefront of the art of DJing. A proof of these skills can be understood by reading the list of winners of the early editions of the *Disco Mix Club (DMC)*. In 1985, the first edition of the DMC, organised by Tony Prince took place at the *Hippodrome*, and quickly became the most important DJ competition, with British DJs dominating from the start.

In the inaugural competition, Roger Johnson won, show-casing a set mixing *Play that Beat Mr. D.J.* by G.L.O.B.E. & Whiz Kid with *Sucker D.J.* by Dimples D., *Gettin Money* by Dr. Jekyll & Mr. Hyde and James Brown.

The competition was initially conceived as a mixing battle, but it took a completely different turn when DJ Cheese introduced the Scratch techniques in his set in 1986, modifying the future course of *DMC*. In 1987 an English DJ, Chad Jackson, won the title, followed by the American DJ Cash Money in 1988. In 1989, with an impressive showcase, Cutmaster Swift won the world title, demonstrating original techniques like the *Copycat*, which later became an international standard.

Cutmaster Swift ▶ A strong introduction is crucial for any DJ; if you don't start off right, you'll quickly lose your audience's attention. I always aim for an exciting beginning. It could be the introduction of a popular record, a catchy chorus hook, or even a dynamic sound effect I create. The key is to maintain that energy, whether through scratches, juggles, or lyric cutting. My routine involved mixing an RnB record with a popular Hip Hop track while performing a victory dance as the ultimate intro. It was a hit! The routine continued with various innovative techniques, including the copycat and body tricks, all within a 6-minute performance.

MC Mello ▶ Dance played a crucial role in the evolution of Hip Hop in the UK. What's significant is that Popping originated from Oakland and LA on the west coast, while Breaking and Hip Hop itself came from the Bronx and New York on the east coast. In London, we experienced the fusion of the west coast and east coast styles, making us a melting pot where both coasts converged in the heart of London, creating a big impact!

Simon Reynolds ▶ Initially all these music scenes whether it was Reggae, or Hip Hop, they really looked to the source. It is very much imitating the Jamaican or American sound, and not doing it that well usually, or better being quite good but not having the sound right, it wasn't that polished luxury sound, that kind of gloss the original production had. Inevitably a little later you would have people who wanted to produce tracks that sounded English. In the music press, I would always do pieces on British Funk, Brit Soul or the new wave of British Reggae and later Hip Hop.

E=mix ▶ What earned Family Quest a lot of respect was our authenticity. Many MCs at the time were listening to American MCs and trying to imitate the American style, but we didn't carry guns, so we didn't need to rap like we were involved in those activities. We were predominantly British, so we brought our unique British style.

MC Mello ▶ When I began writing Rap lyrics in school, I received a positive response because I wasn't attempting to sound like an American. Instead, I used the rules of rhyming as a Londoner. The same applies to London Posse: they were authentically London, fully embracing their UK identity. You could sense the authenticity in their music; it wasn't an imitation, but an original expression rooted in their culture and experiences.

Bunny Bread ▶ Initially, when we first discovered hip hop, we were imitating everything we saw coming from the States – the fashion, the style, basically everything. We absorbed it like a sponge. It wasn't until later that we realized the importance of creating our own style, something uniquely British. We quickly grasped that concept and embarked on our journey toward the mid-'80s.

DJ Supreme ▶ After signing a record deal with Music of Life, we soon recognized the need to create our own music. I drew upon my own experiences, background, and influences. Coming from a Jamaican household, I was exposed to a lot of Dub, Reggae, Soul, Funk, and also admired UK pop stars like David Bowie, Kate Bush, The Beatles, and John Lennon. I combined elements from my Jamaican background, pop and Funk influences, and even scores from movie music. The fusion of these musical styles, the scratching on records, and the intensity of our lyrical delivery all contributed to a style that was so distinct, it carved out its own path.

Ishmahil Blagrove ▶ It was all about reclaiming our identity. When British artists began rapping with a British accent, when London Posse and Demon Boys started using English accents in their rap, they were taking back their space.

Murray Forman ▶ Hip Hop emerged and evolved, its cultural coding was as "Black music" and it was deemed a legitimate artistic expression of the U.S. urban Black youth experience. It was socially and symbolically coded as primarily a "Black" thing, at least in the beginning. As it was transported and conveyed to international audiences, these codings that surrounded the music and Hip Hop culture preceded it and helped to forge the contexts within which Hip Hop took hold in a place like England. Black youth in the UK understood that Hip Hop was by and arguably for Black youth and situated it (and embraced it) in that light. And as they did this, they merged it with other artistic and musical modes of expression which in the UK in the early 1980s, most definitely included Reggae.

In this context, the affirmation by Richie Rich, a DJ of Radio Kiss FM, becomes particularly significant. In an interview with "Hip Hop Connection" magazine, he stated: "I believe Reggae and Rap are both street music, the same streets that are the core of our upbringing. English Rap naturally has a Reggae sensibility".

Hesmondhalgh and Melville also claim the same concept:

> So the United Kingdom already had its own version of an emancipatory Black practice, a Caribbean-derived cultural formation with music at its epicentre that fostered Black expressivity and organised and channelled critiques of institutional racism and neocolonialism. In other words, sound system culture did for Black British urban populations what Hip Hop did for African Americans. Many Black British clubbers and consumers picked up US Hip Hop but incorporated it into their preexisting diet fo Reggae.[4]

This process, which involves the imitation of an original artistic expression and then the adaptation or adoption of a personal style, modelled by one's audience, represents the natural development of an indigenous music scene and the definition of a specific identity. In the London Hip Hop scene, one of the first voices to stand out in this regard was that of London Posse.

[4] David J. Hesmondhalgh, Caspar Melville, *Urban Breakbeat Culture – Repercussions of Hip Hop in the United Kingdom*, in: *Global Noise: Rap and Hip Hop Outside the USA*, Wesleyan University Press, Middletown 2002, p. 90.

FEAT**U**RING THE

MUSIC OF LIFE SHOWCASE

ROCKING THE RHYMES

Poster for the
Music of Life
label artists'
showcase,
London 1989

THE DEMON BOYZ
From the Northside

M.C. DUKE
Defender of the East

ASHER D & DADDY FREDDY
London's Finest

EINSTEIN
The Lyrical Mind

HIJACK
Serving All Suckers

Tuesday 14th March 1989
at
The Cafe de Paris
Leicester Square
London W1
10pm to 3pm
Over 18's only
Dress: Strictly for
THE HOMEBOYZ
Admission £7 with this Ticket

(Admits 1)

MUSIC OF LIFE

Simon Harris ▶ There was no interest from major record labels in producing Rap music at the time, despite the abundance of talent on the streets. So, we decided to take matters into our own hands and create something new – a new scene.

The Music of Life label didn't start as a Rap label originally. It began when Froggy and I were creating remixes. One of our remixes, *The Real Thing – You to Me Are Everything*, reached number 3 on the UK pop chart, which was a significant achievement. However, we were only paid £200 (about 300 euros) for it, and that seemed off. So, we decided to start our own label. We initially approached Morgan Khan, who had the Streetsounds label, known for its electro series of albums, and he offered us a kind of informal record deal. We began by releasing Soul records and had a couple of successful releases.

Unfortunately, when Streetsounds went out of business, it left us without distribution. So Chris Franz and I (Froggy had left by then) went to Pinnacle Distribution, and they supported us in establishing ourselves as an independent label. That's when I suggested we turn the label into a Rap label, as there were no other UK labels specializing in Hip Hop at the time. Our first record under this new direction was *Deaf Beats 1*, but we faced some challenges in completing it. Our A&R guy, Derek Boland (who wasn't Derek B yet), proposed an idea for a Rap track called *Rock the Beat*. We put Derek in the studio and finished the record, and his track turned out to be the most popular one.

For the second album, we decided to shift our focus from licensing American music (which had been the primary source for our first album) to showcasing more UK artists and giving them a chance to be heard. Derek and I embarked on a search for UK talent. We went on the Mick Allen show on Capital Radio and asked artists to send in their demo tapes. We received numerous submissions, including demos from artists like Demon Boyz, Overlord X, and many others. This marked the beginning of our journey to compile an album of UK Rap music. We named it *Hard as Hell*, and that's how UK Rap started.

The artists signed to Music of Life were incredibly talented, and we considered ourselves fortunate to work with them. We fostered a strong sense of community, akin to Motown on a smaller scale. Our artists collaborated with each other, and there was a lot of cross-collaboration. We were at the forefront of producing British Rap music, featuring artists like Demon Boyz, MC Duke, Hijack, and others.

London Posse

The London Posse were one of the most influential Hip Hop groups and the first to perform in the English style. With the release of *Money Mad* and later the album *Gangster Chronicle*, it was as if they had hit the reset button, erasing the first stage of the scene and ushering in a fresh era of Rap. In 2007, Gangster Chronicle was voted the "best UK Hip Hop album of all time" by the readers of "Hip Hop Connection magazine".

The story of the London Posse began in 1986, when four young Londoners decided to form a group to perform as a support band on *Big Audio Dynamite*'s US tour, the new group led by Mick Jones, former guitarist of The Clash. When they accepted the offer, the group didn't even have a name. They would find it during the tour, almost by chance, because the promoters had no idea what to write on promotional posters and flyers, so they decided to put: *The London Posse plus Dancers*. It was a name that sounded good and liked by all members of the group. Actually, their story began a few months earlier, on the night when Sipho,

a very young beatboxer from East London, performed on the stage of Hippodrome during the *Electro Rock Festival*. His microphone skills immediately caught the attention of Mick Jones and Don Letts, who asked him to feature on their track called *C'mon Every Beatbox*, a revisited version of Eddie Cochran's classic Rock n 'Roll song, included in the album *No. 10, Upping St.*, released in 1986.

Mick Jones, the former guitarist of The Clash and a long-time lover of Hip Hop culture, invited Sipho to join *Big Audio Dynamite* on their promotional tour in England and later in the United States.

Sipho had asked his friends Rodney Panton (aka Rodney P, aka MC Rodie Rock), Jeff Tetteh (aka Bionic) and Billy Ntimih (aka DJ Biznizz, aka Spider B, founder of the Live2Break crew) to join him on this adventure. They had all known each other for a while, frequenting the Covent Garden scene. Moreover, Sipho and Bionic had performed together on TV. However, up until that point, the four had never talked about forming a group.

Bionic ▶ Sipho was invited to go on tour with Big Audio

Dynamite, and he asked the rest of us to join him, although it was mainly him they wanted.

Rodney P ▶ While we were at Mick Jones's house, they realized they needed more than just a beatbox for the tour, so we offered to be a part of it. At that point, we didn't have a name or anything.

Bionic ▶ We quickly came together for the tour with no proper arrangement. We didn't even have a name. Our DJ, Billy, joined us later. When we arrived in the United States, they started calling us the London Posse simply because we were from London.

Rodney P ▶ The tour was an eye-opener and a valuable learning experience, but for me, it felt more like a party because I was still a kid in those days. I was still in school when we began touring, and it was during the second leg of the tour that I left school.

Rodney
P, London
2012

Cover of *London Posse / My Beatbox Reggae Style* by London Posse, 1987

Event flyer featuring Tim Westwood, London Posse, and Faze One

Back in London after a long period in the United States, they released their first debut single *London Posse* for the label *Big Life*. The song reached the eleventh position on the UK independent chart, staying there for a remarkable eleven weeks. On its B-Side there was *My Beatbox Reggae Style*, a track where Bionic rapped over Sipho's beatboxing, accompanied by the scratches of DJ Biznizz. After the release of that single, Sipho and Biznizz left the group to pursue their individual projects: Sipho would work with Derek B and Biznizz would join Tim Westwood on his radio show.

The following year, Rodney P and Bionic released their second single, *Money Mad*, on Tim Westwood's label, *Justice*. That track was a true street anthem that gained significant success among both Rap and Reggae lovers, offering a raw, rough fusion of the two genres and highlighting the connection between Jamaica and England.

In 1989, they switched to *Mango*, a subsidiary of *Island Records*, to release their only album, *Gangster Chronicle*, that *NME* had compared to the explosive power of a molotov cocktail. After the release of two other singles, *Tell Me Something* and *Jump Around*, Mango was absorbed by *Island Records*, and the London Posse moved to *Bullitt Records*, managed by manager Errol *Bull* Samuel. The group began recording a second album, *Ladies Love Roughnecks*, but the project was shelved due to lack of financial resources. They released a handful of singles in 1993, including How's Life In London and Pass Me the Rizla on the *British Underground EP*. They temporarily split in 1995, only to reform in 1996 for their final single, *Style*.

Bionic then teamed up with Stevie Hyper D, entering the Jungle and Drum'n'Bass scene, while Rodney continued to record in the Hip Hop field.

Rodney P ▶ In my early life, I was mostly exposed to Reggae music, which was what I grew up with in my family home. But as I entered my teenage years, I was at that age when you're searching for a sound and a movement that defines you, and that's when Hip Hop came into my life. I heard American Hip Hop tunes on the radio, and we would rap along to them. We'd also create our own little versions of their raps, often using fake American accents. Like many UK MCs, I started my career imitating American styles because we were emulating what we heard, and we hadn't yet developed our own unique style. That came later.

It was when we began making our own records that we started to understand what we wanted to represent as artists and individuals. The real turning point for me came when we released our first single. The philosophy of London Posse was to combine elements of Reggae and Rap from the very beginning. If you listen to our original record, you'll notice that Bionic rapped in more of a traditional Reggae style, while I used a more Hip Hop-influenced style, and we fused these different approaches.

When we visited New York City, we realized that rapping in a fake American accent was counterproductive. What the people in NYC appreciated the most was when we rapped in our natural Cockney and yard accents, something that came naturally to us. This approach was more entertaining for them. So, when we returned from NYC, we adopted a new philosophy and decided to embrace our accents fully. During that time, the Saxon sound system also shared a similar philosophy of creating Reggae music with a UK style. The MCs of the Saxon sound system were well-known worldwide. They represented the UK Black experience, and artists like Smiley Culture and his song *Police Officer* had a significant impact on us in terms of how we wanted to represent ourselves as UK Black artists. We were doing Hip Hop, but it was uniquely UK Hip Hop. As London Posse, we decided to take that same mentality and philosophy and apply it to Hip Hop. I'm a dedicated Hip Hop fan, and I'm passionate about all aspects of Hip Hop, not only musically but also culturally. However, I'm not from the Bronx or Brooklyn Bridge; I'm from London. Therefore, if we were going to represent where we come from, our sound needed to be a bit different. What we knew better than anything else was Reggae music. That's why we ended up creating this hybrid sound that combined Hip Hop and Reggae. It allowed us to stay true to ourselves and what we knew best.

Money Mad

Money Mad represents a track from a new era, the first rap song to mix Cockney and Yardie. The beat is reminiscent of NWA, but in the London Posse's Rap, there is a clear Reggae influence.

Rodney P and Bionic exude a rugged, streetwise persona, mirroring the toughness of London during those years. The track perfectly encapsulates the essence of Boom-bap, the iconic sound of the Golden Age of Rap, all within a British framework. Bionic's vocals represent a fusion of Jamaican influence and the gritty authenticity of London.

Rodney P raps with a New York cadence but retains a distinct Cockney accent. Their unique blend of styles solidifies the idea that Hip Hop found a vibrant home in the heart of the United Kingdom.

Cover of *Money Mad* by London Posse, 1988

Rodney P ▶ When we created songs like *Money Mad*, we combined Hip Hop and Reggae elements while expressing ourselves with our own English accents. It was a fusion of these two genres, infused with our slang, culture, and history. We aimed to make Hip Hop that truly represented us and our background.

We wanted to establish our unique style, which was influenced by the UK and Reggae fashion. We didn't wear baggy jeans or oversized t-shirts; our style was a bit different. This unique blend reflected both our UK and Reggae roots, and we wanted our Hip Hop to reflect that.

When we signed with Big Life, they provided us with a list of potential producers for our record. The only name we recognized on the list was Tim Westwood, who was a friend of ours. So, we decided to work with him. On our way to the studio, we stopped at Dub Vendor in Clapham Junction to buy some 45s, which contributed to the musical elements of the track. Later, we met with

Tim Westwood and an engineer from Jive Records named 'Chuck' New, who worked on early Kool Moe Dee and Jazzy Jeff records. Chuck New played a crucial role in piecing together the instrumental track using the musical elements we had collected. He deserves credit for creating one of my favorite UK Hip Hop rhythms.

In *Money Mad*, Bionic and Rodney P depict a society on the brink of economic collapse, a London where young people were forced to do anything to survive:

I could be a mugger, could be a safe cracker / could be a robber, a hitman or computer hacker.

Rhymes that portray a vicious style all too familiar to the poorest segments of the population, a reality where the need for a dignified life pushes people to their limits and to engage in illegal actions. The references mentioned by Rodney P alluded to a painfully real imagery of drug dealers, pawnshops, and stolen money, while Bionic's lyrics are delivered to avoid any misunderstanding:

In London they're robbing, it's coming like a fashion, from other rappers you'll never hear a word of these things, it's happening in England.

Bionic himself raps a bar that has become an instant classic:

I make it easy, or you can get it hard / gimme your money, your jewellery and your credit card.[5]

[5] Lirics edited by Jimmy Green, in *London Posse: Roughneck Chronicle*: http://jimbojonesconveniencestore.blogspot.com/2009/10/london-posse.html?m=1.

The details of this street background are all included in the first verse, leaving no room for misunderstandings. The most explicit reference to British reality comes in the verse in which Bionic boasts of stealing during the Brixton riots. Also, as we have seen, the two MCs rap with two different flows, light-years apart. These connotations are a perfect synthesis of the cultural amalgamation and the social complexity of London in those years.

Simon Harris ▶ If you compare the first London Posse single *London Posse* to their second single *Money Mad*, you can hear a noticeable difference in Rodney P's approach. In the second record, he still retains a bit of an American flow, rhyming in an American pattern. However, that American influence is gone by the time *Money Mad* is released. *Money Mad* is undeniably British, not only in terms of their voices but also in the content they're rapping about. In the track, Bionic talks about robbing a video from Curry's during the riots. These lyrics could only have been written in the context of London and the UK.

With those siren samples, ground-shaking basslines, and the distinctive downbeat that characterises the track, *Money Mad* sounded more like a Dancehall tune than a Rap record.

As Rodney P says: "The original is much more sound system style".

Rodney P ▶ *Money Mad* was inspired by another tune that was out at the time by Tenor Fly called *Inner Cities*. It was just a Hip Hop version of that really.

Rodney P ▶ Hip Hop was a means for us to express our creativity in terms of art, music, and dance. It also served as a platform for us to convey our social ideas and feelings about the life we were living at the time. While Hip Hop is great for partying, dancing, and having a good time on a Saturday night, it has always been a social movement from the beginning. It allowed us to express our thoughts on how society was impacting us in our daily lives. So, for us, it was more than just a way to party; it was a way to express our experiences and emotions in those times.

In 1989, Bionic and Rodney P participated in an anti-apartheid project alongside with other rappers, forming an all star group called the *Black Rhyme Organization To Help Equal Rights* aka *B.R.O.T.H.E.R.* Their purpose was

Cover of the single *Beyond 16th Parallel* by B.R.O.T.H.E.R., 1989

to record the single *Beyond The 16th Parallel*, released by the 4th & B'way Records. The idea was promoted by the music collective Gatecrash, and the track aimed to spread awareness about the situation in South Africa. The song was a perfect example of how Rap music could be used to raise consciousness and fuel protests. Several years prior, the anti-apartheid movement had established the *Free Nelson Mandela* committee to coordinate the struggles. Several artists and bands had dedicated songs to the cause, like *Free Nelson Mandela*, written by Jerry Dammers, a collaboration between The Sussed and The Specials AKA. Dammers himself was among the founders of the *Artists Against Apartheid* organisation. The single *Beyond the 16th Parallel* featured the participation of Demon Boyz, MC Mello, Cookie Crew, She Rockers, London Rhyme Syndicate, Katch 22, Gunshot, Hijack, Icepick, Overlord X and London Posse. Additionally, Dancehall artists like Junior Reid, Tenor Fly, Ricky Rankin and Tippa Irie joined it, to name just a few.

B.R.O.T.H.E.R. even included Labor Party MP Bernie Grant, opening the song by stating:

As Black people we must smash the 16th parallel, as people we must unite and smash the racist South African government and free South Africa and Namibia. The ANC and SWAPO will win. AMANDLA!

This is the verse of the London Posse instead:

In a South Africa whole heap a shegries a gwan, dey na wan no Black made a trade union, dem a blow up offices and dem a kill off blackman. We affe get militant uprise and stand strong, so listen lyrics straight from the posse that we all made, C.O.S.A.T.U. say what they need is a living wage now! We have to fight for that, build on the Black, so run go record shop and buy this track.

Gangster Chronicle

Gangster Chronicle, the first and only album by London Posse, is undeniably considered the starting point, the origin of UK Rap. Rodney P and Bionic revolutionised the classic expressive canons of American Hip Hop to create an original style, a specific expression of London's reality. Besides the bold linguistic approach, the album was undeniably groundbreaking in its content, with lyrics addressing topics such as shootings, robberies, police intimidation, and sexual conquests. The storytelling of the two young MCs portrayed issues more commonly associated with a *ruffneck* (a street thug) than an up-and-coming rapper. On a musical level, on the other hand, the tracks seamlessly blended James Brown

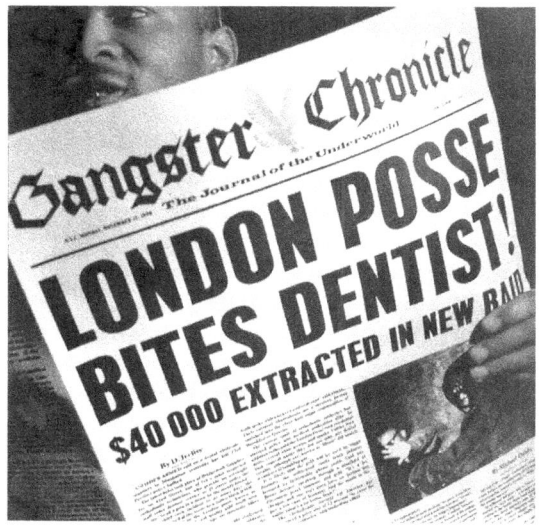

Cover of *Gangster Chronicle* by London Posse, 1990

samples with Dub and Reggae classics, creating an organised confusion reminiscent of the style of Public Enemy. Produced by Sparkii Ski, member of the Jus Badd Crew, DJ Devastate and the group members themselves, the album sounded markedly different from previous Rap productions, solidifying the London Posse's reputation as one of the most talented groups of the British scene.

Rodney P ▶ There was no clear roadmap for how to navigate this music, create it, or release it. We were signed to Big Life, which served as both our label and management, leading to potential conflicts of interest. Initially, we experienced some success, but it began to taper off. We had to seriously ponder whether we wanted to pursue this music career. Sipho and Billy (DJ Bizznizz) ventured into other projects, leaving me and Bionic to determine if we wanted to press on. We had a vision for the sound we wanted, but we lacked the studio expertise. Neither of us were studio wizards. We had to reach out to people who understood our musical aspirations. Additionally, we needed a label to release our work. Fortunately, we connected with Mango through Island Records. Our album marked a turning point in UK Hip Hop. Many believed it would sound unimpressive in English, but we didn't sound insincere when conversing in our day-to-day lives, so there was no reason for it to sound contrived when we put the verses together neatly. In fact, what came across as inauthentic was us rapping in American accents.

Bionic raps this in *Oversized Idiot*:

I ain't a US replica, I don't emulate / the rhymes I generate penetrate, then you make / noise cos you know my voice is that of / a London Black man that can rap...

Sparkii Ski ▶ We represented the second generation of UK Hip Hop. As artists, we had already developed our own identity, drawing heavily from our experiences with Reggae sound systems, where we initially performed. So, we were shaping our style in that context. Often, people only consider the Reggae influence in Hip Hop as pertaining to the music and MCing, but it goes beyond that. It's about sound system culture and high-fidelity audio.

The British sociologist Les Back, while identifying various similarities with African Americans in terms of economic deprivation and racial marginalisation, emphasised how Black Londoners "looks out and plots cultural connections with African Americans, while at the same time looking in and reconstituting the local aesthetics of South London. The language and style of South London are thus laced with symbols and cultural fragments from urban America and the Caribbean that are rearranged in a unique way".[6] The group managed to effectively catch their audience with a direct, unfiltered language, like street poetry capable of reflecting the variety of hybrid sounds that characterised London, as well as all cities with a strong Black presence. Part of the allure of the London Posse stemmed from the way they had chosen not only to represent themself within their urban context, but also to include the voices of the

[6] William "Lez" Henry, Les Back, *Reggae Culture as Local Knowledge: Mapping the Beats on South East London Streets*, in William "Lez" Henry e Matt Worley (a c. di), *Narratives from Beyond the UK Reggae Bassline: The System is Sound*, Palgrave MacMillan, Londra 2020, p. 65.

community they belonged to, giving those tracks a sense of authenticity without precedents, indissolubly linking them to a place and a specific era.

In *Original London Style*, Rodney P raps:

> I come from London / So when I put up the twang / Some just can't understand the slang and the lingua.

With these lyrics, the MC underlines the outsider status of the London Posse, precisely because of the choice to use local slang. Although it was undeniably Rap music, the language generated confusion and set them apart from all the other groups that had not yet found their own identity. Hip Hop, Black English and urban slang: an incredible mashup. At the beginning of the *Original London Style* video, there is a female voice introducing the song, saying: "They're always turnin' out with these new words, cockneys, in't they? What's the new one??". This question highlights how language is a living entity, capable of changing and evolving according to the period and place. The London Posse moved with extreme ease between different voices and dialects, claiming Cockney as part of their inheritance, providing themselves and their fans with the opportunity to reinvent themselves through music.

For the mainstream media and the police, Cockney and Patois were associated with crime and poverty. In the track *Live Like the Other Half Do*, they harshly criticised the media representation of Black people and the racist practices of the London police.

> Another day of racist police brutality And this reality is changed my personality.

B-boy Extravaganza
Meets Rap Attack
con London Posse e
MC Mello, Paradiso -
Amsterdam, 1993

The lyrics of the two MCs provided, for the first time, a sort of context from which to draw in order to understand and confront the social and political dynamics of racism. For example, in this track, there is a direct reference to special police laws called *Sus*. By addressing issues like unemployment, drugs, girls, money and street life, the London Posse conquered considerable resonance throughout the country. Those rhymes helped spread ideas that reflected the diasporic nature of Hip Hop culture, also highlighting elements of race and class that strongly characterised the experiences of an entire generation.

In *How's Life in London*, released in 1993, they celebrated their status as Londoners, but at the same time they pointed out that London was a very distant city far removed from the one advertised for foreigners and tourists. The video of the song opens with a close-up of Big Ben accompanied with the familiar sounds of the city, before a quick cut frames a TV presenter who, with an authoritative voice, announces: "BBC World News presents This Is London".

The subsequent frames show a group of young Black men staring defiantly at the camera. In just a few moments, a famous tourist attraction like Big Ben was transformed into a mysterious territory to most, but well known by those living in the outskirts. That shot also represented a multiracial and multicultural city, a very different London, that deviated from traditional standards and played a significant role in the search for a shared identity among Black teenagers.

As Murray Forman writes in *The Hood Comes First*, providing visual representation is an attempt to connect specific urban aesthetics with a well-recognized space. The views of housing estates, street scenes, chants, gangs and fights all highlight the importance of the place of origin.

> Check my grammar / The girls in Japan love the slang / And the ones in Manhattan they like the chattin'.

These rhymes strongly assert that Hip Hop has now become an international phenomenon that transcends all boundaries.

Sparkii Ski ▶ Rodney P and Bionic had this amazing ability to write their lyrics on the spot in the studio. Bionic had a significant influence on Rodney P in many ways, especially on the creative side. Bionic was the instigator, the explosive genius. He would write the hooks, come up with song ideas, and even decide on the song titles...

Flyer for the N.W.A.'s concert at Brixton Academy on June 9, 1991, featuring London Posse, Demon Boyz, and MC Mello

DJ Devastate ▶ They had this amazing ability to write their lyrics on the spot, record them in the booth, and then listen back to improve them even further. It was truly astonishing; they had an abundance of lyrics and were masters of clever wordplay. Rodney and Bio had an endless supply of lyrics, and they were incredibly skillful with their wordplay.

The drum programming, samples, and mixing were incredible, considering the low budget available. A large part of the album was improvised, constructed and formulated around the basic ideas and records that the duo brought into the studio. Even the samples were also created on the spot, along with the rhythm and the rest of the beat. This was Sparkii's standard, who produced almost the entire album.

However, things were different when the London Posse collaborated with *Twilight Firm* – Brian B and DJ Devastate.

DJ Devastate ▶ It was right after the *Recognition* LP. Both Demon Boys and London Posse had inked deals with Mango Records, under the management of Erroll Samuels, who was like the Rush Management of the UK, handling a stable of talented artists. I had struck up a good relationship with Rodney and Bionic because I truly admired their work. Whenever we met, they were always receptive to what we, Demon Boys, and our production team, Twilight Firm, were doing. So, I was determined to collaborate with them.

At some point, Rodney and I exchanged numbers, and we had discussions about them wanting us to produce some tracks for their LP. Rodney was residing in South London, Battersea, while we were based in Tottenham. They would drive all the way to Tottenham to listen to the beats we were working on. I decided to create something special for them, and Rodney mentioned he was looking for some energetic, rolling beats akin to the track *Vibes*. I had a clear idea of what I wanted to do and which break I was going to sample. I wanted to hear them rap over a traditional hip-hop track that blended seamlessly with their distinctive style.

So, I created the track *Jump Around*. I sampled a break by Marvin Gaye, chopped it up, and added some drums. I also incorporated chopped horns from three different records. My brother and I pieced together this collage of horns, using a 303 Roland, and Brian handled the bassline programming. It's quite astonishing that the version that was eventually released wasn't even properly mixed. Rodney and Bionic laid down their lyrics, and before we knew it, the track was out there.

Rodney P ▶ It was precisely the kind of Hip Hop flavor we were aiming for. We recognized the need for one of those energetic party Hip Hop tracks, and they were the group crafting that sound, particularly in the UK club scene. Believe me, we were devoted Hip Hop enthusiasts, and we wanted to demonstrate that we could deliver that style. When I first listened to the tune, it was a significant moment, and when we played that track, we were thrilled.

With the London Posse, more than any other group, the scene placed the Black British experience at the centre of the Atlantic diaspora, engaging in a dialogue between British Black communities, the United States and Caribbean, without ever privileging a single voice.

Simon Jones ▶ Hip Hop has been a sustaining force in Black British culture, but it has also been reshaped and reinterpreted by Black youth in Britain to address British realities and the Black experience. The appeal and significance of Hip Hop vary across generations. Older generations of Black Britons, especially those who grew up in the 1960s and 1970s, have a strong connection to Reggae culture. However, the 3rd and 4th generations show a deeper affinity for Hip Hop culture, which they have adapted, transformed, and fused with elements of Reggae and other dance music forms to create styles like Grime. Hip Hop culture flows into Grime, and Reggae elements like DJing and toasting play a part too. At the core of British Hip Hop is Rap, the art of spontaneously delivering lyrics over rhythmic tracks. Rap's adaptability and versatility allow it to be applied to local conditions, experiences, and various forms of repression and racism that manifest in different contexts.

Murray Forman ▶ It surely did help to enforce (or maybe inform and inflect) Black British culture. It served and continues to serve as an amplifier of a sort, presenting a new creative, artistic medium through which to define the Black British experience and to articulate not only the grievances, despair, fury, mourning, anger, affront, and resistance but also as a site for innovation, a medium for play and humour and ribald performance, a storytelling medium, and a mode of sharing affect and the sustaining aspects of love and nurture. Black communities in the UK and elsewhere employ Hip Hop's creative apparatuses and practices in all these ways as a means of sharing, connecting, and that important Hip Hop concept: building.

30 Years Later

Fraggle ▶ Hip Hop was pure love. You'd rush home from school, lock yourself in your bedroom, listen to LWR, and practice on linoleum or cardboard, all alone. It was all about the love for it. There was no money involved; it was the sheer passion that fueled you.

Fresh Ski ▶ I'd choose the title of a track from one of our singles, titled *Incredible*, because that's exactly what the scene was at that time – incredible. To describe those days using other words? It was devastating, it was unifying, and, well, it was just... yeah, it was amazing.

Mystery MC ▶ I can't imagine what my life would have been like without Hip Hop, and many other kids who were part of it would probably say the same. I had so much inside me that needed an outlet. I was going

Mystery MC (Family Quest), London 2012

through a challenging phase back then, and Hip Hop was my anchor. What's fascinating is that it wasn't supported by the adults; it was our peers, other kids our age, who believed in it. We knew it was going to progress because it was so incredibly powerful.

Bunny Bread ▶ We quickly grasped the essence of it. Once we understood what Hip Hop was all about, we wholeheartedly embraced it, making it our own.

Dizzi Heights ▶ This music originated from the impoverished ghettos of America, and it found its way to our own disadvantaged neighborhoods. From there, we propelled it into the mainstream. What makes this music beautiful is that it provided a means for people who might not have had a voice otherwise to express themselves.

Pride ▶ The remarkable thing was that young people, without any formal training, rehearsals, or cues, could come together and unleash a level of creativity that was truly unparalleled. It was quite extraordinary.

Fraggle ▶ The legacy we've left behind is the transformation of many clubs. They used to pay us for performances but didn't let us mingle with others. We were there to perform, but gradually, it became acceptable to have Black people in West End clubs. Our legacy is that you can go clubbing anytime you want without being told, "You can't come in here".

Yankee ▶ The first word that comes to mind is "Unity" because that's precisely what Hip Hop brought – a sense of unity among people from diverse backgrounds.

Linton Lee ▶ In our youth, we were brimming with excitement and energy. It was an incredible experience to meet, jam, communicate, and express ourselves. Hip

Bunny Bread

Hop provided an outlet for every aspect of young people's creativity, from dancing to making music, and even just having meaningful conversations. It truly was something magical.

James McNally ▶ I don't want to idealize it, but this Hip Hop scene was like a little utopia for many young guys and girls. It offered an escape from whatever troubles they were facing in their neighbourhoods, schools, or families. The Hip Hop scene allowed them to redefine their lives and identities, fostering predominantly positive relationships with their peers and channelling their energy in a constructive manner.

MC Duke ▶ We paved the way for them to follow. Derek B, MC Duke, Demon Boys, London Posse, and all the crews active during that time, including the Cookie Crew, Wee Papa Girl Rappers, and She Rockers, blazed the trail for the new generation of British MCs. Without our presence, there would be no MCs today, no Dizzy Rascals.

Simon Harris ▶ The legacy of UK Hip Hop is that it has become a global phenomenon, and it's finally gained widespread recognition as a vital part of the international music scene. Artists in America now eagerly seek collaborations with their UK counterparts. It's an honor to have been part of the early stages of this movement.

MC Mello ▶ Hip Hop culture encourages self-expansion and personal greatness. It taught us to take care of ourselves and each other. This is especially crucial in a society that's torn by economic hardships, racism, and prejudice. During times when societal divides are widening, this movement emphasizes unity, regardless of one's background or circumstances. Without a culture or movement capable of inspiring and influencing individuals, we would be left with uninspired generations. An uninspired youth can be destructive, while an inspired one can change the world. Hip Hop played a significant role in pushing us to transform our world.

Rodney P ▶ We should be grateful for those days because, fortunately, they have given us what we have today. In the UK, we've evolved beyond just Hip Hop; we now have Drum and Bass, Garage, Grime, and other music scenes. All of these movements trace their roots back to the Bronx and the influence of Kool Herc, a Jamaican originator. The global seeds he sowed have led us to where we are today. We appreciate the music, the vibes, and the culture that is Hip Hop.

Rodney P ▶ That was the mentality of us UK Hip Hop kids, Unstoppable, we were unstoppable, we were young, stupid, energised, and Hip Hop was the soundtrack to our life.

Reference Bibliography

Andy Wood, *London Posse and the Birth of British Hip Hop*, in "Atlantic Studies", 6, 2009.

Caspar Melville, *It's a London Thing: How Rare Groove, Acid House and Jungle Remapped the City*, Manchester University Press, Manchester 2019.

David Hesmondhalgh, Caspar Melville, *Urban Breakbeat Culture: Repercussions of Hip-Hop in the United Kingdom*, in Tony Mitchell, *Global Noise: Rap and Hip Hop Outside the USA*, Wesleyan University Press, 2002.

Dick Hebdige, *Cut 'n' Mix: Culture: Identity and Caribbean Music*, Routledge, London 1990.

Dick Hebdige, *Subculture: The Meaning of Style*, Routledge, New York 2016.

Henry Louis Gates Jr., *A Reporter at Large: Black London*, in Kwesi Owusu (a c. di), *Black British Culture and Society: A Text Reader*, Routledge, London-New York 2000.

John Hind, Steve Mosco, *Rebel Radio: The Full Story of British Pirate Radio*, Pluto Press, London 1985.

Les Back, *New Ethnicities and Urban Culture: Social Identity and Racism in the Lives of Young People*, Taylor & Francis Ltd, London 1996.

Lloyd Bradley, *Bass Culture. When Reggae Was King*, Penguin, London 2000.

Lloyd Bradley, *Sounds Like London: 100 Years of Black Music in the Capital*, Serpent's Tail, London 2013.

Paul Gilroy, *There Ain't No Black in the Union Jack*, Routledge, London 1987.

Paul Gilroy, *The Black Atlantic. L'identità nera tra modernità e doppia coscienza*, Meltemi, Milano 2003.

Raymond Codrington, *The Homegrown: Rap, Race, and Class in London*, in Kamari Maxine Clarke, Deborah A. Thomas (a c. di), *Globalization and Race: Transformations in the Cultural Production of Blackness*, Duke University Press, 2006.

Simon Jones, Paul Pinnock, *Scientists of Sound: Portraits of a UK Reggae Sound System*, Bassline Books, London 2018.

Simon Jones, *Black Culture, White Youth: The Reggae Tradition from JA to UK*, Macmillan, London 1988.

Simon Jones, *Rocking the House: Sound System and DJ Cultures*, in "Journal of Popular Music Studies", vol. 1, n. 2, 1995.

Stuart Hall, Tony Jefferson, *Resistance Through Rituals: Youth Subcultures in Post-War Britain*, Routledge, London-New York 2006.

Trevor Phillips, Mike Phillip Windrush, *The Irresistible Rise of Multi-Racial Britain*, HarperCollins Publishers, London 1999.

Acknowledgments

In concluding this project, I would like to express my gratitude to Marcyliena Morgan, Director of the Harvard Hiphop Archive & Research Institute, Henry Louis Gates Jr., Director of the Hutchins Center, the Department of African and African American Studies at Harvard, as well as Lidia Ravviso, Viola Vatrini, Nicola Cavalazzi, and the entire *Unstoppable* crew. Without them, this book most likely would not exist.